READER'S DIGEST

CROCHET
GIFTS FOR THE HOME

55 Step-by-Step Projects

ANGELA KING

D1411224

Reader's
Digest

READER'S DIGEST ASSOCIATION INC.
Pleasantville, New York / Montreal

ABBREVIATIONS

	AMERICAN	BRITISH
approx	approximately	
beg	beginning	
CC	contrasting color	
ch	chain	
cm	centimeter(s)	
col	color	
cont	continue	
dc	double crochet	treble crochet
dec	decrease	
dia	diameter	
dtr	triple double	triple treble
foll	following	
g	gram(s)	
grp	group	
hdc	half double crochet	half treble crochet
inc	increase	
L	left	
LH	left hand	
lhs	left-hand side	
m	meter(s)	
MC	main color	
mm	millimeter(s)	
no.	number	

	AMERICAN	BRITISH
opp	opposite	
patt	pattern	
PC	popcorn	
prev	previous	
quad tr	quadruple triple	quintuple treble
quin tr	quintuple triple	sextuple treble
R	right	
rem	remaining	
rep	repeat	
RH	right hand	
rhs	right-hand side	
rnd	round	
RS	right side	
sc	single crochet	double crochet
sl st	slip stitch	
sp(s)	spaces(s)	
sq(s)	square(s)	
st(s)	stitch(es)	
tog	together	
tr	triple	double treble
ttr	triple triple	quadruple treble
WS	wrong side	
yo	yarn over	yarn round hook

Pine furniture, china, and glass featured in the photographs
by courtesy of Country Pine & Collectibles,
Sidmouth Street, Devizes, Wiltshire, England

A READER'S DIGEST BOOK
Edited and produced by David & Charles

First published in the UK in 1993
Copyright © Text and line illustrations Angela King 1993, 1997
Photographs by Di Lewis

Printed in the UK by Butler & Tanner Ltd.

Library of Congress Cataloging in Publication Data

King, Angela.
 [55 crochet gifts for the home]
 Crochet gifts for the home : 55 step-by-step projects /
Angela King.
  p.   cm.
 First published in Great Britain in 1993 under the title:
55 crochet gifts for the home.
 Includes index.
 ISBN 0-89577-968-4
 1. Crocheting—Patterns. 2. House furnishings.
3. Household linens. 4. Gifts. I. Title.
TT820.K525 1997
746.43′4—dc21   97-13240

Contents

Introduction · 4

Notes · 6   Techniques · 7
Filet Crochet · 11   Sewing and Trimming · 15
Blocking and Pressing · 15

CHAPTER ONE—THE HALL · 17
Filet Curtain · Table Runner · Purse · Flowerpot Cover · Shawl · Bag · Women's Gloves

CHAPTER TWO—THE LIVING ROOM · 29
Key Bookmark · Lamp Shade · Playing Cards Envelope · Sofa Throw · Antimacassar
Picture Frame · Afghan · "Windows" Pillow · Needlecase · Doily · Place Mat

CHAPTER THREE—THE KITCHEN · 45
Ice Cream Cone Border · Coffee Jar Cover · Egg Cozy · Simple Rug · Filet Jam Jar Cover ·
Filet Shelf Edging · Pitcher Cover · Pot Holders · Plant Hanger

CHAPTER FOUR—TEA TIME · 57
Lace Doily · Tray Cloth · Tablecloth · Cake Band · Tea Cozy · Napkin Rings

CHAPTER FIVE—THE BEDROOM · 69
Bedspread · Hot Water Bottle Cover · Filet Bed Linen Edgings · Dressing-table Set ·
Tabletop or Chest Cover · Small Cushion

CHAPTER SIX—THE BATHROOM · 81
Toilet Tissue Cover · Bathmat · Filet Guest Towel Edging · Small Curtain ·
Lavender Bags · Tissue Box Cover

CHAPTER SEVEN—THE NURSERY · 89
Filet Bassinette Trim · Canopy and Ruffle · Dress · Baby Jacket · Bonnet · Baby Shawl

CHAPTER EIGHT—CELEBRATION · 101
Ribbon · Bell · Christmas Ball · Christmas Tree Decorations · Christmas Angel · Snowman ·
Basket · Floral Card · High-wheeler Card

EDGINGS, BRAIDS, AND INSERTIONS · 117

YARN MANUFACTURERS · 127   INDEX · 128

Introduction

Of all the traditional crafts, crochet must be one of the most versatile. It can be used to make a wide range of beautiful items, including objects for the home, clothing, jewelry, flowers, toys, containers, and trimmings for all types of other needlework; I've even seen a crocheted hammock and a crocheted chess set!
Crochet is quick to do and can be applied both decoratively and practically. In addition to the huge assortment of commercial yarns available, you can use wire, string, cord, ribbon, or even dyed pantyhose cut spiral-fashion into two continuous lengths.

Bearing in mind the usefulness and versatility of crochet, we have arranged this book in chapters that invite the reader to take an imaginary tour through a house, stepping first into the hall, then the living room, and so on, room by room, with a variety of gifts carefully laid out in each. In the hall you will find a pair of gloves and a filet curtain; in the bedroom, a pillowcase edging and pretty

mats for a dressing table; you can pause to enjoy tea time, and then discover a lacy crocheted shawl for a new baby in the nursery. In some rooms you may care to stop and linger awhile and be inspired to make one of the gifts displayed there.

Throughout the book, the patterns have been graded according to difficulty—so whether you've enjoyed crochet for years or are just getting started, there will be a project to suit your ability. To help you decide which of the many designs to tackle, look for ✿, which indicates "easy"; ✿✿, "some experience necessary"; or ✿✿✿, a "challenge."

There is variety, too, in the scale of projects, which range from a sofa throw made with traditional Granny squares down to little decorations for a Christmas tree. Some of the designs are nostalgic, like the antimacassar; some more modern, such as the bath mat. There are also both "light" and "heavy" styles—for example, the lacy cotton doily and the kitchen shelf trim. Trimmings—edgings, braids, and insertions— are also included toward the end of the book. Hooks used range from size 8 to size J/10, and each pattern gives measurements in both standard and metric, while abbreviations and their equivalents in British crochet books are explained.

While I was designing the projects for this book, it occurred to me that although many women can sew and knit, far fewer can crochet. Many wish they had the ability but either have not found the time to learn, are deterred by their belief that it is difficult, or have become discouraged soon after starting and have given up. With this in mind, I have included a techniques section especially for the beginner,

in which I've tried to ensure that both text and diagrams are absolutely clear and simple to follow. The stitch count given for each of the basic stitches will further facilitate learning. Also included are basic filet crochet instructions, in which a knowledge of the crocheted chain and double crochet stitch is all that's required. Here, I've tried to explain not only the method of working filet but also how to go on to create your own unique designs.

If you really want to be able to crochet though, then keep at it. Practice, and if you come up against a hurdle, be determined and don't give up. It will be well worth it, for once you have mastered a few basic stitches all sorts of lovely crochet patterns can be achieved simply by combining the stitches in different ways.

Notes

1 Gauge is the number of sts and rows to equal a given measurement: in this book it is usually calculated over 4 inches (10cm), and has been specified for all patterns where essential or important to the completed size of an article. The gauge is especially useful when a particular yarn is discontinued or unobtainable. Buy one ball of your chosen yarn and make a sample to see if the fabric produced is attractive. Alter the hook size, if necessary.

2 The **yarns** needed for projects in this book are specified first by *type*—e.g. "a size crochet cotton," with the specific brand used for the original item named in ( )s. Ideally, you should buy that brand. However, this is not always possible, and so we have specified the total *length* used (or purchased), rather than the amount in weight, since the length contained in two balls of the same weight can vary considerably. This is even more true in the case of knitting yarns. The closest American equivalent to a British "double knitting" yarn, used for some of these projects, is knitting worsted; however this is noticeably thicker than double knitting, and 2 ounces (57g) of knitting worsted will contain fewer yards (meters) than the British yarn. If the label of your chosen yarn does not give the length, ask the salesperson to help you estimate the quantity you will need.

If possible, purchase all the yarn required for an article at one time, and check the labels to make sure that the dye number is the same throughout. A difference between dye lots can be very noticeable.

3 Use only the best quality **hooks**. These should then last for years, and will be an advantage to the learner. (See table below.)

4 Multiples. At the start of some of the instructions in this book, it states: (Ch x, or any no. of ch divisible by . . .). This is an indication that the article or trimming can be made to any size required.

A length of ch divisible by 10–2 means any multiple of ten minus two—for example, ch 28 (= 30–2); ch 38 (40–2); or ch 48 (50–2); and so on. In this book it does not mean divisible by 8. Therefore, a length of ch divisible by 6 + 2 will be any number that can be divided by 6, with 2 added on—for example, 50ch, 62ch, and so on.

5 Basic **crochet techniques** sometimes differ to a small degree, and it is important to understand two of the variations in particular:

(i) A turning ch may not always count as the 1st st of a row, but is sometimes made only to bring the hook into line for the start of a new row. With a straight piece of crochet of 10sts, all 10sts after the turning ch—from the 1st st to the 10th st—will be worked into. There-fore, at the end of a row, the previous row's turning ch will not be worked into.

(ii) On the 1st row of crochet, the positions for initial insertion of the hook are consecutive and therefore easy to remember. For example, 1sc into 2nd ch from hook (the skipped ch positioning the 1st dc); 1hdc into 3rd ch from hook; 1dc into 4th ch from hook, and so on (the skipped chs forming a st). Instructions for initial hook placement do not al-ways agree, but patterns will state which ch st to employ.

While learning to crochet, you will find it helpful always to count the sts of each row.

◆

USEFUL ITEMS

For working crochet:
Safety pins for use as markers and for holding pieces together for seaming
Small, sharp scissors
Ruler and coiled steel rule
Large tapestry needle (blunt) for threading thick yarns
Medium-size plastic bag to keep yarn clean while in use—knot opening, leaving space for yarn

For finishing:
Needles: sharp-pointed sewing and crewel (embroidery) needles; blunt-pointed tapestry needles
Small cotton cloth
Spray bottle

A GUIDE TO EQUIVALENT HOOK SIZES								
These equivalents are approximate. Always check your gauge, and change hooks if necessary.								
Metric	**U.S.**		**Metric**	**U.S.**		**Metric**	**U.S.**	
0.60	14 (steel)		2.00	B/1 (aluminum or plastic)		5.50	I/9 (aluminum or plastic)	
0.75	12	,,	2.50	C/2	,,	6.00	J/10	,,
1.00	10	,,	3.00	D/3	,,	6.50		
1.25	8	,,	3.50	E/4	,,	7.00	K/10½	,,
1.50	7	,,	4.00	F/5	,,	8.00	11	,,
1.75	4	,,	4.50	G/6	,,	9.00	13	,,
			5.00	H/8	,,	10.00	15	,,

Techniques

Learning to crochet is much easier at the very beginning if you use either a light to medium-colored size 3 cotton or a sport-weight yarn, with a size F/5, G/6 or H/8 crochet hook. Left-handed crocheters should reverse L and R instructions.
(N.B. In some illustrations the hook has been omitted for clarity.)

◆
CHAIN (ch)

Make a slipknot and insert hook. Tighten loop enough for it to slide easily on the main part of the hook. Keep the knot fairly tight.

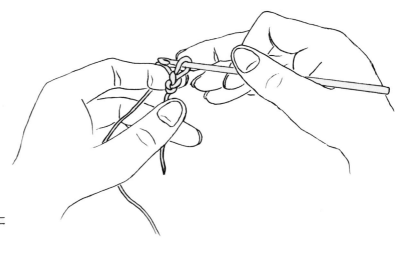

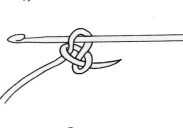

Allow the upper part of the hook to rest between thumb and first finger. Temporarily hold top of slip loop in position with the second finger, right hand.
Wind yarn from ball over hook (yo) with the left hand. Maintain control of the yarn by slightly gripping it between both second and third fin-

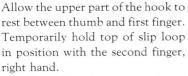

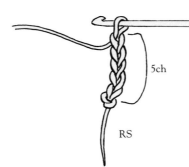

5ch

RS

1 2 3 4 5

WS

ger, and closed fourth finger of same hand. (You may discover a more comfortable method of controlling the yarn for yourself, in time.) Hold knot with thumb and first finger, left hand, and draw the yarn through loop on hook. One chain stitch made (1ch).
Hands should be in a relaxed position, but in control of hook and yarn. Again, temporarily hold in position top of loop on hook (not counted as a stitch), yo, and complete another ch st.
Altogether, make 5ch—called "chain 5."
Right side (RS) of the base chain (sometimes called "foundation chain") is facing. Now turn work over to look at wrong side (WS) of chain. Note the center, horizontal line of loops.

SLIP STITCH (sl st)

Retain the 5ch made.

Slip stitch (sl st) is a shallow stitch used mostly for joining or shaping. Insert hook into 2nd ch from hook, under top two strands of yarn. Yo. With one movement, draw yarn through both the 2nd ch from hook and loop on hook. 1sl st made.

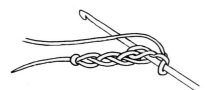

The first ch st was skipped; the second ch was worked into, therefore 3ch remain unworked.

Work 1sl st into each of remaining 5ch. 4sl st made. (If you have any difficulty inserting the hook, the chains may be too tight; this can easily be remedied by using a size larger hook for the chains and reverting to the original hook for foll rows.)

SINGLE CROCHET (sc)

Ch 5.

Row 1: Insert hook into 2nd ch from hook (always under top two strands of yarn, unless otherwise stated). Yo, draw yarn through. There are two loops on hook.

Yo again. Draw yarn through both the loops on hook. 1sc made. Insert hook into next ch, yo, draw yarn through, yo, draw yarn through both loops on hook. 2sc made. Sc to end by working 1sc into each of remaining 2ch. 4sc made. RS is facing.

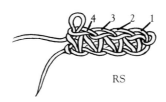

RS

In all, 4sts have been worked. Skipping the 1st ch helps to position the 1st sc. The hook could also initially be inserted into the 3rd ch from hook. Here the 2 skipped ch would *form* the 1st sc. In both cases, the 1st sc row has one fewer sts than the base ch. The foll rows are worked in the same way.

Row 2: Ch 1 and turn the crochet, or turn and then make the 1ch, so that WS is facing. (It is rather awk-

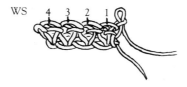

WS

ward to insert hook into the 1st st on rows, so one—or more—turning ch counts as the 1st st of a new row.)

After the turning ch, insert hook into 2nd st and make 1sc. Work 2sc to end of row, turn.

Row 3: Make 1ch for 1st st, 1sc into each of next 3sts, turn.

The last st worked into will be the 1st st (turning ch) of the previous row.

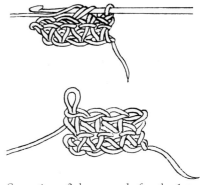

Sometimes 2ch are made for the 1st sc, and whether 1ch or 2ch are used depends mainly on tension and/or yarn being used. (Try loosening the loop on hook before making the 1ch, and notice any difference.) Work another few rows of sc on the 4sts. Try inserting hook under only one strand (either top back or top front.) You will note that this produces a slightly different effect.

FASTENING OFF

Finish your crochet by fastening off. To do this, break the yarn (leaving enough of the yarn for darning in), and draw the end through the loop on the hook.

HALF DOUBLE (dc)

Ch 5.

A half double crochet is taller than a sc, so the hook is inserted into the 3rd ch from hook, and at the end of rows you will have to make 2ch to turn.

Row 1: Yo, insert hook into 3rd ch from hook. Yo, draw yarn through, yo, draw yarn through all 3 loops on hook. The 2 skipped ch sts have formed the 1st hdc, so 2hdc have been made.

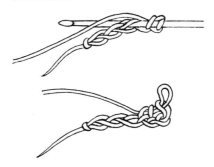

Yo, insert hook into next ch, yo, draw yarn through, yo, draw yarn through all 3 loops on hook. Work 1hdc into next st (last ch). 4hdc made. The 1st hdc row has one st fewer than the base ch.

Row 2: Ch 2 for 1st hdc. Inserting hook under the two strands on top of the st, work 1hdc into each of next 3sts. The last of these sts is worked into 2nd ch of the 2ch of the previous row.
Rep Row 2 twice more. Break yarn and fasten off.

◆

DOUBLE CROCHET (dc)

Ch 5.
A double crochet is the tallest of the 3 basic sts, so the hook is inserted into the 4th ch from hook, and 3ch made to turn. Note that there are 3 "stages" in making a dc.

Row 1: Yo, insert hook into 4th ch from hook, yo, draw yarn through, yo, draw yarn through 2 of the 3 loops on hook, yo, draw yarn through the 2 remaining loops on hook. The 3 skipped ch sts have formed the 1st dc, so 2dc have been made.
Work 1dc into last st.
The 1st dc row has two fewer sts than the base ch.
Turn, and ch 3 for the 1st dc.
Row 2: 1dc into next st (hook under top two strands at left of center).

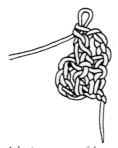

Work 1dc into top of last st. This last st was formed from the ch sts skipped on Row 1. Turn.
Work two more rows in dc. Break yarn and fasten off.

◆

TRIPLE CROCHET (tr)

Ch 5.

Row 1: Yo twice. Insert hook into 5th ch from hook, yo, draw yarn through, yo, draw yarn through 2 of the 4 loops on hook, yo, draw yarn through 2 of the 3 loops on hook, yo, draw yarn through 2 loops on hook. 2tr made. Turn.

Row 2: Ch 4 for 1st tr. Yo twice, complete 1tr into next st (top of 4 skipped base ch), 2tr made. Break yarn and fasten off.

◆

TRIPLE DOUBLE (dtr)

Ch 14.
Row 1: Yo 3 times, insert hook into 6th ch from hook, yo, draw yarn through, yo, draw yarn through 2 of the 5 loops on hook, yo, draw yarn through 2 of the 4 loops on hook, yo, draw yarn through 2 of the 3

loops on hook, yo, draw yarn through the 2 rem loops on hook. Dtr to end (10 sts).
Taller double triples can be made similarly, simply by altering the no. of times the yarn is wound around hook and drawing yarn through 2 loops at a time as before. The following table gives the no. of times the yarn is wound around hook. Try working a row of each of these stitches.

dc	1
tr	2
dtr	3
tr tr	4
quad tr	5
quin tr	6, etc.

◆

TURNING CHAINS

Usual no. of ch made for the 1st st of a row.

sl st	1 (or work the 1st sl st into 1st st of row)
sc	1 (or 2, often dependent on yarn thickness)
hdc	2
dc	3
tr	4
dtr	5
tr tr	6
quad tr	7
quin tr	8, etc.

See Note 5, p. 6.

◆

DOUBLE CHAIN

This can be used as an attractive cord or as an alternative base ch.
Ch 2. Work 1sc into 2nd ch from hook, inserting hook under top strand only. *Work 1sc into last sc

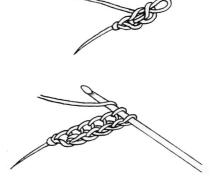

made, inserting hook under single strand at left of sc.

Rep from * to desired length. Break yarn and fasten off.

◆

INCREASING

This is achieved simply by working 2 or 3 sts into one st of previous row. To increase at row ends, work the increase into the 2nd st from each end.

9sts
7sts

This helps maintain neat edges on the crochet. A contrasting thread can be used temporarily to mark increases so that they are easily seen.

To increase more than 2sts at the beg of a row, make a ch for each st required, plus 1ch for sc or hdc, 2ch for dc, and so on. For an increase of 5dtr, therefore, ch 9.

Start the next row as you would after a base ch, and work 1sc into 2nd ch from hook, or 1tr into 5th ch from hook, etc.

To increase more than 2sts at the end of a row, extend the relevant row by joining on a separate piece of yarn with a sl st, make a number of ch sts to equal the number of sts

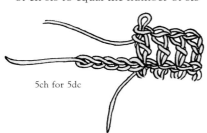

5ch for 5dc

required, and draw yarn end loosely through last ch st to secure. (Or make one extra ch st, draw end through, and pull to tighten.)

◆

DECREASING

A decrease can sometimes be made by simply skipping a st, although this may leave a noticeable hole. A better method is to work 2sts (or more) together.

sc2tog: Insert hook into next st, yo, draw yarn through, insert hook into foll st, yo, draw yarn through, yo, draw yarn through all 3 loops on hook.

sc3tog: As sc2tog but work over next 3sts, instead of 2sts, and draw yarn though all 4 loops on hook.

hdc2tog: Yo, insert hook into next st, yo, draw yarn through, yo, insert hook into foll st, yo, draw yarn through, yo, draw yarn through all 5 loops on hook.

hdc3tog: As hdc2tog but work over next 3sts, instead of 2sts, and draw yarn through all 7 loops on hook.

dc2tog: Yo, insert hook into next st, yo, draw yarn through, yo, draw yarn through 2 of the loops on hook, yo, insert hook into foll st, yo, draw yarn through, yo, draw yarn through 2 of the loops on hook, yo, draw yarn through all 3 loops on hook.

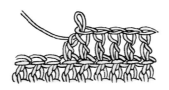

dc3/4/5/6tog: As dc2tog but work over next 3/4/5/6sts, and draw through all 4/5/6/7 loops on hook.

tr2tog: *Yo twice, insert hook into next st, yo, draw yarn through, (yo, draw yarn through 2 loops on hook) twice*.

Rep from * to *, yo, draw yarn through all 3 loops on hook.

To decrease at ends of rows, work the decreases into sts next to ends to maintain neat edges.

The process of working sts together is also used for creating many lacy patterns as well as for decreasing.

◆

CIRCLES

(Example 1: sc)

Ch 4. Join with sl st into circle (inserting hook into 1st ch made, yo, and drawing yarn through both 1st ch st and loop on hook to make sl st). (4sts.)

Round 1: Ch 1 to start this round. (The 1ch puts the 1st sc on the outside of the circle.) Work 8sc (twice number of ch) into circle, that is, over 4ch into center space of circle.

Skip 1ch, sl st into 1st sc. (8sts.) The foll rounds can be worked in two ways. Either make separate rounds with 1ch for 1st sc and close each round with sl st into this st, or make continuous rounds, omitting the ch and working around in a spiral manner.

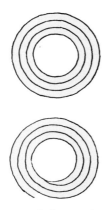

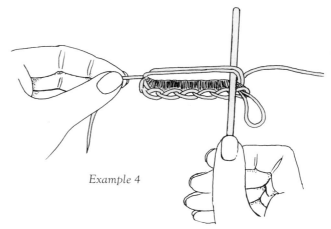

Example 4

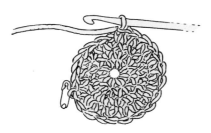

RS is facing, and the work is not turned at end of each round. (When working in a spiral, use a marker to indicate the last st of each round.)

Round 2: Ch 1 for 1st sc, 1sc into same place as 1ch, 2sc into each foll st to end, sl st into 1st sc. (8sc increased = 16sts.)

Round 3: Ch 1 (1st sc), 2sc into next st, *1sc into next st, 2sc into next st. Rep from * to end, sl st into 1st sc. (24sts.)

Round 4: Ch 1 (1st sc), 1sc into next st, 2sc into next st, *1sc into each of next 2sts, 2sc into next st.

Rep from * to end, sl st into 1st sc. (32sts.)

Round 5: Ch 1 (1st sc), 1sc into each of next 2sts, 2sc into next st, *1sc into each of next 3sts, 2sc into next st. Rep from * to end, sl st into 1st sc. (40sts.)

Round 6: Ch 1 (1st sc), 1sc into each foll st to end, sl st into 1st sc. (40sts.)

(Example 2: dc)
Ch 4. Join with sl st into circle.

Round 1: Ch 3 (1st dc), work 11dc into circle (= 3 times number of ch), sl st into top (3rd ch from hook) of 3ch.

Round 2: Ch 3 (1st dc), 1dc into same place as 3ch, 2dc into each foll st to end, sl st into top of 3ch. (24sts.)

Round 3: Ch 3 (1st dc), 2 dc into next st, *1dc into next st, 2dc into next st. Rep from * to end, sl st into top of 3ch. (36sts.)

(Example 3: sc)
Ch 2.

Round 1: 7sc into 2nd ch from hook.

Round 2: Work 2sc into each sc.

Round 3: *1sc into next sc, 2sc into next sc.

Rep from * to end.

(Example 4: sc)
Wind yarn twice around finger. Insert hook into space, and draw yarn through to front. Ch 1, and work sc over the 2 strands. Close circle by unhooking last loop, placing hook temporarily into circle, and pulling on the free end.

◆

CHANGING COLOR

Work the last stage of a stitch in the next color you wish to use, so that the loop on the hook is in the new color.

FILET CROCHET

Filet crochet consists simply of doubles and chains (worked as blocks and spaces) to form a variety of patterns. Numerous household and fashion items can be made with filet crochet, and it is relatively easy to create personalized designs of letters, shapes, flowers, and even complete pictures by setting out a

pattern similar to an ordinary crossword puzzle. The crochet is then worked following this chart. Each horizontal line represents one row. Each vertical line on a row represents one double crochet. Each space between these vertical lines can be filled in with two more doubles (for a block) or two chains (for a space).

The first row begins at the bottom right-hand corner, the second (even) row is worked from left to right, the third (odd) row from right to left, etc. To begin a row with a space, make 5 extra ch, and work 1dc into 8th ch from hook. To begin with a block, make 3 extra ch, and work 1dc into 4th ch from hook.

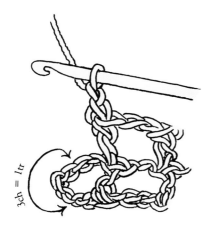

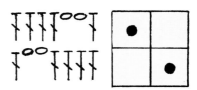

Blocks and
Spaces

KEY: dc $\textbf{T}$ ch $\textbf{O}$

Place last dc in correct place to retain vertical edge of the filet crochet.

The 5 extra ch stand for 1dc + 2ch; the 3 extra ch for 1dc. To determine the number of ch sts to begin with, count the squares across, × 3 (1dc and 2ch for each sq) + 5 (3 for 1dc + 2ch sp), or 3 (dc block).
Therefore, the pattern for a filet background with, say, 15 spaces across × 2 spaces high, reads as follows:
Ch 50.
Row 1: 1dc into 8th ch from hook, *2ch, skip next 2ch, 1dc into next ch. Rep from * to end, turn.
Row 2: Ch5 (1st dc and sp), 1dc into

next dc, *ch 3, skip next 2ch, 1dc into next dc.
Rep from * to end.
Filet chart "A" (see below) begins:
Ch 45.
Row 1: 1dc into 4th ch from hook, 1dc into each of next 2ch, *ch 2, skip next 2ch, 1dc into each of next 4ch.
Rep from * to last 3ch, ch 2, skip next 2ch, 1dc into last ch, turn.
Row 2: Ch 5 (dc + 2ch), *skip next 2ch, 1dc into next dc, ch 2, skip next 2dc, 1dc into next dc, ch 2.
Rep from * omitting last 2ch at end of row.

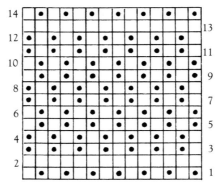

Chart A

When a block falls over a space, the 2dc are worked into the space.
The appearance of the crochet will improve if each block or space is square. This can be difficult to achieve, but it is not always essential. Try experimenting with different yarns and hook sizes, or vary your working tension.
It is useful to have graph paper for making the designs; 1/10-inch (2mm) square should enable you to see the overall picture clearly. On a very few occasions it may be advisable to elongate the design on the graph if relatively square blocks and spaces are an impossibility. You would need to work and measure a small sample of blocks and spaces using the desired yarn first in order to correct any deficiency on graph paper. For example, a

A rose—from sketch to a filet chart

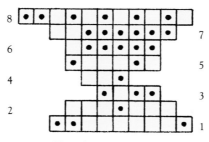

Chart for practice piece

design that may be 5sqs wide and 5sqs long and in the right proportion on the paper, may need to be redrawn as 5sqs wide and 6 or 7 sqs long.

The lacet is a stitch that can look extremely pretty when incorporated into filet crochet. It is worked with a 5ch "bar" over two squares and two rows.

On the 1st lacet row, instead of filling two squares with the usual dcs or leaving sps, ch 3, skip 2ch or 2dc, 1sc into next dc, ch 3, skip 2ch or 2dc, and then work 1dc as usual.

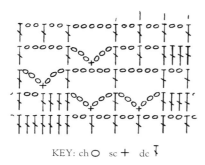

KEY: ch O   sc +   dc †

On the return two, make a bar of 5ch over the V-shaped lacet.

To work a lacet over a bar, simply work the sc into 3rd ch of the bar, or a dc into this center ch when reinstating the squares.

Filet can also be made using trs and extra chs, or with other variations. It could be worked from side to side rather than from base to top. Charts can be used to design pointed or scalloped filet crochet edgings. These edgings are worked from the narrow end and shaped by increasing or decreasing the blocks or spaces at one end of a row.

◆

PRACTICE PIECE FOR SHAPING IN FILET CROCHET

Ch 30.

Row 1: 1dc into 4th ch from hook, 1dc into each of next 2ch, (ch 2, skip next 2ch, 1dc into next ch) 6 times, 1dc into each of next 6ch, turn.

Row 2: Block dec at beg and end of row: 1sc into 1st st (last dc made), 1sl st into each of next 3dc, ch 5 (= 1st dc + 2ch), skip next 2dc, 1dc into next dc, (ch 2, skip next 2dc, 1dc into next dc) twice, 2dc into next sp, 1dc into next dc, ch 2, skip next 2dc, 1dc into next dc) 3 times, turn.

Row 3: Sp decs at beg and end of row: 1sl st into 1st st, 1sl st into each of next 2ch, 1sl st into next dc, ch 3, (2dc into next sp, 1dc into next dc) twice, ch 2, skip next 2dc, 1dc into next dc, 2dc into next sp, 1dc into next dc, turn.

Row 4: Sp inc at beg and block decs at end of row: ch 7 (= 2ch base, ch 3 for dc, 2ch top), 1dc into 1st st (last dc of prev row), ch 2, skip next 2dc, 1dc into next dc, 2dc into next

sp, 1dc into next dc, turn.

Row 5: Sp and block inc at beg; block inc at end of row: ch 10, 1dc into 8th ch from hook, 1dc into each of next 2ch, 1dc into 1st dc, ch 2, skip next 2dc, (1dc into next dc, ch 2, skip next 2ch) twice, 1dc into next ch (top of 3ch dc), do not turn. 1tr (yarn twice over hook) into same ch as last dc made, 1tr into base of tr. To complete the block inc, work 1tr into base of tr just made, turn.

Row 6: Ch 5 (1st dc + 2ch), skip 1st 3tr, 1dc into next dc, (2dc into next sp, 1dc into next dc) 3 times, 1dc into each of next 3dc, 2dc into next sp, 1dc into last dc (5th ch), turn.

Row 7: Block inc at beg and sp inc at end of row: ch 5, 1dc into 4th ch from hook, 1dc into next ch, 1dc into 1st dc, 1dc into each of next 15dc, ch 2, skip next 2dc, 1dc into next dc, ch 2, 1dtr into same place as last dc made, turn.

Row 8: 2 block inc at beg and sp inc at end of row: ch 8, 1dc into 4th ch from hook, 1dc into each of next 4ch, 1dc into dtr.

Follow chart to end.

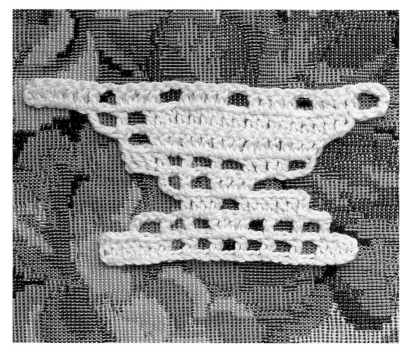

Practice piece for shaping in filet crochet.

♦

SOME MORE FILET PATTERNS

SEWING AND TRIMMING

The following stitches are used for articles that require some sewing or embroidery.

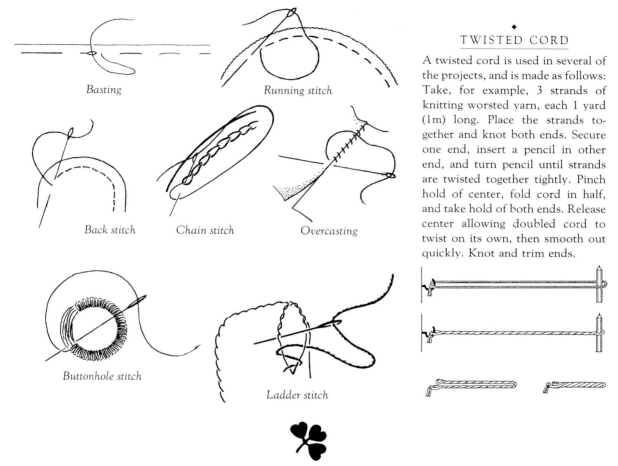

Basting

Running stitch

Back stitch

Chain stitch

Overcasting

Buttonhole stitch

Ladder stitch

♦

TWISTED CORD

A twisted cord is used in several of the projects, and is made as follows: Take, for example, 3 strands of knitting worsted yarn, each 1 yard (1m) long. Place the strands together and knot both ends. Secure one end, insert a pencil in other end, and turn pencil until strands are twisted together tightly. Pinch hold of center, fold cord in half, and take hold of both ends. Release center allowing doubled cord to twist on its own, then smooth out quickly. Knot and trim ends.

BLOCKING AND PRESSING

This is an important process, to which a great deal of time and care should be given.

Blocking simply means pinning out an article to its correct shape and size prior to pressing. Pin crochet, RS down, on a clean, padded surface, such as an ironing board or table, depending on the size of the article. Insert pins so that they slant slightly outward.

For pressing, first read the instructions on the yarn label. This should indicate whether or not to use an iron and, if so, its heat setting and if a damp or dry cloth is required.

Very useful for blocking and pressing is a spray bottle, which can be purchased inexpensively. Alternatively, use any thoroughly cleaned-out sprayer that has a spray lever and screw top attachment for filling. Lightly spray crochet, or cover with a damp cloth, and leave for a few hours to dry before removing pins. (A spray bottle is also invaluable when a "damp" cloth is indicated on the yarn label, because a spray can dampen a cloth to the right degree without soaking it.) If pressing is absolutely necessary, use a clean iron, and "press" rather than "iron," employing a light up-and-down action. Avoid the pins, which could scratch the iron's surface.

CHAPTER ONE

The Hall

Flowerpot Cover (page 21); Table Runner (page 19);
Filet Curtain (page 18).

FILET CURTAIN

This filet crochet curtain, with its unusual galleon design, is ideal for covering a hall window while still letting in daylight.

MATERIALS

3,000 yards (2,750m) of a size 5 crochet cotton
(yarn shown: Twilleys Southern Comfort
Crochet Cotton)
Size C/2 (2.50mm) hook
Spray starch for pressing (optional)

GAUGE

8 sqs wide and 8½ sqs long = 4 inches (10cm) sq

MEASUREMENTS

Approx 42 × 79 inches (117 × 200cm)

INSTRUCTIONS

Each space for this curtain is formed with 1tr, 3ch, 1tr: the 3ch space is changed to 3tr to form a block of 5tr. Ch 7 (tr + 3ch) for a space or ch 4 (tr) for a block at the beg of a row: at a row end, work the last tr into 4th of 4ch or 7ch (see below). For further instructions on filet crochet, see page 11. Start by chaining 344 (85 × 4 = 340 + 4).

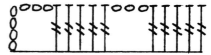

From left to right, ch 7 for 1st space. 5 tr and 3ch form the filet blocks and spaces for the curtain.

Row 1: 1 tr into 5th ch from hook, 1tr into each foll ch to end, turn.
Row 2: Ch 7 (tr + 3ch sp), (skip next 3tr, 1tr into each of next 5tr, ch 3) twice, skip next 3tr, *1tr into next tr, ch 3, skip next 3tr.
Rep from * to last 17sts, (1 tr into each of next 5tr, ch 3, skip next 3tr) twice, 1tr into last tr. Cont by following the chart from 3rd row (odd rows worked from R to L).
Rep the last 2 rows of chart until curtain measures approx 79 inches (195cm), or desired length. The final few rows can be folded back to make a casing.

TABLE RUNNER

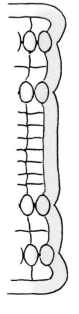

Perfect for dressing up a sideboard, this table runner is made all the more attractive by the large spaces worked into it.

◆

MATERIALS

283 yards (260m) of a size 10 crochet cotton
(yarn shown: DMC Cebelia No. 10)
Size 4 steel (1.75mm) hook

◆

GAUGE

37 tr = 4 inches (10cm) across

◆

MEASUREMENTS

Approx 23 × 9½ inches (58 × 24cm)

◆

INSTRUCTIONS

Ch 226 (or any no. divisible by 6 + 4 for length).
Row 1: (RS) 1tr into 5th ch from hook, 1tr into each foll ch to end, turn.
Row 2: Ch 13 (tr + 9ch), skip 1st and next 5sts, 1tr into next st, *ch 9, skip next 5 sts, 1tr into next st.
Rep from * to end, turn.
Row 3: Ch 4 (tr), 3tr into 1st tr, *ch 2—fairly loosely, 3tr into next tr.
Rep from * to end, working 4tr instead of 3tr into last tr (4th of 13ch), turn.
Row 4: Ch 4 (tr), tr3 tog (next 3 sts of 1st grp), *ch 4, 1sc under next 9ch and 2ch loops tog, ch 4, tr3tog of next grp.
Rep from * to end, working tr4tog for last grp, turn.
Row 5: Ch 9 (tr + 5ch), 1tr into top of 2nd tr grp (slightly left of center), *ch 5, 1tr into top of next tr grp.

Rep from * to end, turn.
Rows 6–9: Rep rows 2–5 once more.
Row 10: Ch 9 (tr + 5ch), 1tr into 2nd tr, *ch 5, 1tr into next tr.
Rep from * to end, turn.
Rep last row 5 times more, and Rows 2–5 twice more. Break yarn and fasten off. Rejoin to 4th of 9ch at beg of last row.
Final row: Ch 4 (tr), *1tr into each of next 5ch, 1tr into next tr.
Rep from * to end.

◆

EDGING

Do not turn—work alongside. Note that there are 14sps and 4 "acorns" alongside (see below).
Work 7tr into 1st sp, 1sc into center (side) of 1st acorn, 5tr into next sp, 3tr into st before next sp, 5tr into 3rd sp, 1sc into next acorn center, 6tr into 4th sp, (1tr into st before next sp, 3tr into next sp) 6 times, 1tr into st before next sp, 6tr into 11th sp, 1sc into 3rd acorn center, 5tr into next sp, 3tr into st before next sp, 5tr into next sp, 1sc into next acorn center, 7tr into last sp, 1sc into single loop at base ch corner.
Work a row of sc into single loops at base ch edge.
Complete opp sides to match, ending with 1sl st.

14 spaces and 4 "acorns" are formed along the shorter sides of the table runner.

PURSE

 *Quickly made, this dainty purse with its shamrock emblem would make a nice gift— perhaps as a memento for March 17, St. Patrick's Day.*

MATERIALS

450 yards (410m) of size 5 crochet cotton (yarn shown: Twilleys Southern Comfort Crochet Cotton)
Optional 2nd color for cord
Size B/1 (2.00mm) hook
2 beads with fairly large holes for threading onto cord ends
Crewel needle
Green embroidery floss
Sewing needle and thread

GAUGE

19sts and 21 rounds = 4 inches (10cm)

MEASUREMENTS

3½ × 3¼ inches (9 × 8.5cm)

INSTRUCTIONS

Starting at base, ch 64. Join with sl st into circle. Work 1sc, under top loop only, into each ch st for 1st round, and 1sc into top back loop of each foll sc, until 2¾ inches (7cm) from base. (Follow slanting line of sts from slipknot to indicate where to end.)

EYELETS

*Ch 2, skip next 2sts, 1sc (both loops) into each of next 2sts.
Rep from * to end. Replace the skipped sc on next round by working 2sc into each 2ch sp, and cont in sc (top back loops) on the 64 sts for another ⅓ inch (8mm). Work 1sl st under both loops into next st.

EDGING

Row 1: Ch 4, skip next 3 sts, 1sl st (both loops) into next st.
Rep from * ending with 1sl st into base of 1st 4ch.
Round 2: Work 6sc into each 4ch sp. Sl st into 1st sc. Break yarn and fasten off.

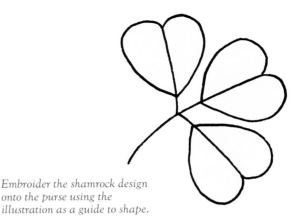

CORD

Ch 160. Work back along ch with 1sl st into 2nd and each foll single horizontal loop behind each st. Sew in all ends.

Turn purse WS out and flatten, with slipknot at side. Join yarn to side of base and close base with sl st through both edges, but work into only 4 alternate pairs of sts at each side (to gather), and then into each rem pair.

Embroider small shamrock on one side (see right). Thread cord through eyelets. Fit beads onto cord ends and sew in place.

Embroider the shamrock design onto the purse using the illustration as a guide to shape.

FLOWERPOT COVER

Even if you aren't lucky enough to have a green thumb, you can work this lovely floral gift to cover a flowerpot on a windowsill or sideboard.

MATERIALS

285 yards (260m) of a size 10 crochet cotton in main color (MC) (yarn shown: DMC Cebelia No. 10 (sufficient for a 5½-inch- [14cm-] tall pot with base and top dias of 5 inches [13cm] and 5½ inches [14 cm])
1 or more contrasting colors (CC) for stems, leaves, and flowers
Size 4 steel (1.75mm) hook
Matching sewing thread
Sewing needle

INSTRUCTIONS

Make a length of ch with MC to fit, slightly stretched, around base of pot. Join the untwisted ch into a circle with 1sl st.

Round 1: Ch 3 for 1st dc, 1dc into each foll ch to end, 1sl st into top of 1st dc. (For 5-inch- [13cm-] dia pot base = approx 126ch/126dc.)

Cont in rounds of dc to one round above height of pot. Fit cover onto pot every now and then and make gradual increases, in varying positions, as necessary.

Fold final round back onto outside, over prev round. Ch 1, and work an edging round of sc, inserting hook through both sps between dcs of last 2 rounds. Work 1sl st at end and fasten off.

STEMS

Measure the top circumference of pot, and make two ch lengths in CC, each half this measurement. Make 4 of each size leaf for a larger pot, and 4 small and 4 medium for a small pot.

SMALL LEAF

Ch 12 in CC, 1sc into 2nd ch from hook, 1hdc into each of next 4ch, 2hdc into each of next 2ch, 1hdc into each of next 3ch, 1sc into end ch.

Ch 1, place slipknot yarn end behind, then beg and ending with the 1sc, work back along base ch, following instructions in reverse (i.e., 1sc, 3hdc, etc.). Sl st at end into skipped ch at tip. Break yarn and fasten off. Sew in ends.

MEDIUM LEAF

Ch 14 in CC, 1sc into 2nd ch from hook, 1hdc into each of next 2ch, 1dc into each of next 3ch, 2dc into each of next 2ch, 1dc into each of next 3ch, 1hdc into next ch, 1sc into end ch.

Ch 1, place slipknot yarn end behind, then beg and ending with the 1sc, work back along base ch, following instructions in reverse (i.e., 1sc, 1hdc,

3dc, etc.). Sl st at end into skipped ch at tip. Break yarn and fasten off. Sew in ends.

LARGE LEAF

Ch 16 in CC, 1sc into 2nd ch from hook, 1hdc into next ch, 1dc into each of next 2ch, 1tr into each of next 3ch, 2tr into each of next 2ch, 1tr into each of next 3ch, 1dc into next ch, 1hdc into next ch, 1sc into end ch.

Ch 1, place slipknot yarn end behind, then beg and ending with the 1sc, work back along base ch, following instructions in reverse (i.e., 1sc, 1hdc, 1dc, etc.). Sl st end into skipped ch at tip. Break yarn and fasten off. Sew in ends.

FLOWERS

For a small flowerpot, make only 2 small flowers; a larger pot requires 2 of each, with 1 complete flower being made by placing the small flower over the larger one.

For a large flower, ch 6 in CC. Join with sl st into circle.

Round 1: Ch 1, 12sc into circle, sl st into 1st sc.

Round 2: Ch 1, 1sc into same place as ch, 2sc into each rem st, sl st into 1st ch.

Round 3: *Ch 7, 1sc into 2nd ch from hook, 1sc into each rem ch, 1sc into next sc on circle. Rep from * working last sc into 1st of 7ch.

For a smaller flower, work as large flower to end Rnd 1, then rep Rnd 3 but working 5ch instead of 7ch petals. Sew in all ends. Retain a slight point at tip of leaves.

Appliqué two similar designs of leaf and stem on each half of cover using sewing thread. Start with one stem approx 2 inches (5cm) from rim and ending approx 1½ inches (3cm) from base. (Begin the second stem an inch or so [few cms] before end of first stem.) Attach flowers by sewing around center circles, leaving petals free. Make design according to pot size, using illustration as a rough guide (see below).

The illustration shows the smaller flower placed over the larger, the stem, and one pair each of small, medium, and large leaves.

SHAWL

A very simple method of increasing creates the long, triangular shape of this lovely old-fashioned shawl.

MATERIALS

1,200 yards (1,100m) of knitting worsted (yarn shown: Sirdar Country-Style Double Knitting)
Size H/8 (5.00mm) hook

GAUGE

7hdc/7sps and 12 rows = 4 inches (10cm) sq

MEASUREMENTS

(Excluding fringe) across top 59 inches (1.5m); center length 34 inches (86cm); sides 44 inches (112cm)

INSTRUCTIONS

Starting at base point, ch 6 and join with sl st into circle.

Row 1: Ch 5, into circle work (1hdc, ch 2) twice and 1hdc, turn. (3sps.)

Row 2: Ch 5, (1hdc, ch 2) into each of 1st 2 sps, (1hdc, ch 2, 1hdc) into last sp, turn. (4sps.)

Row 3: Ch 5, (1hdc, ch 2) into each sp to last sp, (1hdc, ch 2, 1hdc) into last sp, turn. (5sps.)

Rep last row until 99sps across top.

Do not turn—cont by working along 2 sides: 1sl st into sp of last loop worked, ch 6 (dc + 3ch), 1hdc into next 5ch loop, ch 3, 1dc into next hdc loop, ch 3. Work this patt, with (1hdc, ch 3) into each 5ch loop and (1dc, ch 3) into each hdc loop, along both sides of shawl. At base point, work (1dc, ch 3) twice into the 6ch circle. Turn.

Cont with two more rows, but work only (1hdc, ch 3) into each loop, (1dc, ch 3) twice into new base loop, and (1hdc, ch 3) twice into final loop of 1st row. Omit last 3ch of 2nd row.

Break yarn and fasten off.

Cut 16-inch (40cm-) lengths of yarn for fringe. Fold 5 of these together at center (4 strands can be used, but the finished effect will not be as dense), insert fold into a 3ch loop on the shawl, and thread ends through. Pull ends to make a fairly tight knot.

Rep for all 3ch loops. Trim ends.

BAG

✲ ✲

This highly textured handbag or small shopping bag is very pretty for summertime and functional, too.

MATERIALS

540 yards (495m) matte-finish sport-weight cotton (yarn shown: Twilleys No. 1 Handicraft Cotton)
Size G/6 (4.50mm) hook
Large snap fastener
Matching sewing thread and needle
Lining fabric (optional)
2 × 11-inch (28cms) (approx) dowel or lengths of cane (optional)

GAUGE

Over dc—14sts and 7½ rows = 4 inches (10cm) sq

MEASUREMENTS

12 inches (30cm) sq

INSTRUCTIONS

(Make two pieces.)
Ch 45.

Row 1: 1dc into 4th ch from hook, 1dc into each foll ch to end, turn.

Row 2: Ch 3 (1st st), 1dc into each foll st to end, turn. (43sts in Rows 1–8.)

The Hall

Row 3: Ch 2 (1st st). With hook horizontal, work 1dc in front and around 2nd and each foll dc of last row, turn (see below).

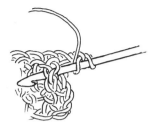

Hook placement for "dc around dc," beginning at Row 3

Row 4: Ch 2 (1st st). Work 1dc into 2nd and each foll dc of Row 2, working final dc into same st as last 2ch, turn.
Row 5: As Row 3, working final dc around 1st st of last row, turn.
Row 6: Ch 2 (1st st). Work 1dc into 2nd and each foll dc of Row 4, working final dc into same st as last 2ch, turn.
Row 7: As Row 3, working final dc around 1st st of last row, turn.
Row 8: Ch 2 (1st st). Work 1dc into 2nd and each foll dc of Row 6, working final dc into same st as last 2ch, turn.
Row 9: Ch 2 (1st st), (1dc, ch 2, 1sc) into 2nd st, * skip next 2sts, (1dc, ch 2, 1sc) into next st.

Shawl (page 23); Women's Gloves (page 26), and Bag (page 23).

Rep from * to last dc and 2ch start of prev row, skip 1dc, 1 hdc into top of 2ch, turn.

Row 10: Ch 2 (1st st), (1dc, ch 2, 1sc) into 1st 2ch sp, *(1dc, ch2, 1sc) into next 2ch sp.

Rep from * to last 2sts, skip 1st, 1hdc into last st, turn.

Rows 11–14: Rep last row 4 times more.

Row 15: Ch 3, 1dc into 1sc, *1dc into next 2ch sp, 1dc into each of next 2sts.

Rep from * to last 2ch sp, 1dc into sp, skip next st, 1dc into last st, turn. (43sts.)

Rep Rows 2–6, Rows 9–15, and Rows 2–8.

Break yarn and fasten off. With the rows of bag running vertically, sew together base and 2 sides.

HANDLES

Using yarn doubled, make 4 × 10ch pieces for handle loops. Sew to bag at open edge: one piece to 1st and 3rd dc "stripes" and another to 6th and 8th stripes on one side of bag. Rep for 2nd side. Sew in all ends. Make a handle using double ch st (p. 9) with 33 feet (10m) of yarn. Thread through 2 loops on lhs and 2 loops on rhs of bag. Join into circle. Machine-stitch loop ends and handle-join for added strength if wished. Line if desired. If using dowels or cane, leave lining hems open at one end for removal before laundering.

Sew snap at center, near top of bag.

WOMEN'S GLOVES

❋❋

 A silky-look yarn and small open pattern give these gloves a luxurious feel.

MATERIALS

540 yards (495m) of a size 5 crochet cotton (yarn shown: Twilleys Galaxia 5)
Size B/1 (2.00mm) hook
Sewing needle

GAUGE

1sc, 3ch patt worked 12 times
+ 1sc = 4¾ inches (12cm) across
12 rows = 1¼ inches (3cm)

MEASUREMENTS

To fit average-sized hands

INSTRUCTIONS

Starting with back of left-hand glove at 4th finger side, ch 93.

Row 1: 1sc into 9th ch from hook, *ch 3, skip next 3ch, 1sc into next ch.

Rep from * to end, turn.

Row 2: Ch 4 (sc + 3ch), *skip next 3ch, 1sc into next dc, 3ch.

Rep from * to last loop, skip 3ch, 1sc into next st, turn.

Rows 3–6: Rep last row 4 times more.

Row 7: Ch 4, skip next 3ch, 1sc into next sc, (ch 3, 1sc into next sc) 14 times. Ch 40 for 3rd finger.

Row 8: 1sc into 9th ch from hook, (ch 3, skip next 3ch, 1sc into next ch) 7 times, ch 3.

Work the patt (Row 2 from *) to end, turn.

Rows 9–14: Rep Row 2, 6 times more.

Row 15: Ch 4, 1sc into next sc, (ch 3, 1sc into next sc) 15 times. Ch 40 for 2nd finger.

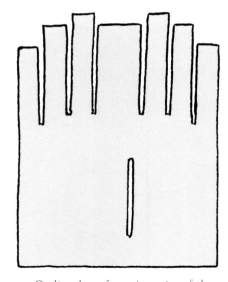

Outline shape for main section of glove

Row 16: As Row 8.

Rows 17–22: Rep Row 2, 6 times more.

Row 23: As Row 15 but ch 36 for 1st finger.

Row 24: 1sc into 9th ch from hook, (ch 3, skip next 3ch, 1sc into next ch) 6 times, ch 3, skip next 3ch.

Patt to end, turn * *.

Rows 25–36: Rep Row 2, 12 times more.

Row 37: Ch 4, 1sc into next sc, (ch 3, 1sc into next sc) 3 times, ch 31, skip next 7sc, 1sc into next sc. Patt to end, turn.

Row 38: As patt—work the (ch 3, 1sc) patt along the 31ch.

Rows 39–40: Patt 2 more rows.

Rows 41 and 42: Rep Rows 15 and 8.

Rows 43–48: Patt 6 rows.

Row 49: Rep row 15 but ch 36 for 3rd finger.

Row 50: Rep Row 24.

Rows 51–6: Patt 6 rows.

Row 57: Rep Row 7 but ch 32 for 4th finger.

Row 58: 1sc into 9th ch from hook, (ch 3, skip next 3ch, 1sc into next ch) 5 times, ch 3, skip next 3ch.

Patt to end.

Rows 59–63: Patt 5 rows.

Break yarn and fasten off. Sew in ends.

◆

RIGHT-HAND GLOVE

Work as for left glove to * *, then rep Row 2 twice and Rows 37 and 38 once.

Patt 12 rows.

Cont from Row 41 to end.

Fold gloves, matching fingers, with RS inside. When wearing completed gloves, wrist edges will slightly curl onto wrists, although either side of fabric could be chosen as RS.

◆

SIDE AND FINGER JOINING

(Note: Along any ch st edges, work into sc on nearest row.)

Beg at open side at wrist, join yarn to 1st st on 1st (nearest) side and ch 1. Insert hook into 1st st on 2nd (farthest) side, yo, draw loop through 2nd side, yo, draw through both loops on hook to complete 1sc. Ch 3, 1sc into next sc on 1st side, insert hook into next (equivalent) st on 2nd side, completing 1sc as before, ch 3. Cont along side, ending with ch 3 and without working last corner sc. Gather top by working 3sc evenly across top of finger. Cont joining as on side until both sc at 4th finger base have been worked together. Make 1sc into sc at base of 3rd finger on 1st side and 1sc into base on 2nd side, ch 3.

Seam all fingers in the same way. Ch 1 at finish to secure.

Break yarn and fasten off. Sew in ends.

◆

THUMB

This is made separately.

Ch 28.

Row 1: 1sc into 8th ch from hook, *ch 3, skip next 3ch, 1sc into next ch.

Rep from * to end, turn.

Row 2: Ch 4, skip next 3ch, 1sc into next sc.

Patt to end, turn.

Row 3: Ch 11, 1sc into 8th ch from hook, ch 3, skip next 3ch, 1sc into next sc.

Patt to end, turn.

Rows 4–7: Rep last 2 rows twice more. (12 loops.)

Rows 8–11: Rep Row 2, 4 times more.

Row 12: Patt to last 2 loops, turn.

Row 13: Ch 4, skip next 3ch, 1sc into next sc.

Patt to end, turn.

Rep last 2 rows twice more.

Break yarn, gather short, straight edge for top of thumb, and sew in ends.

Fold thumb RS inside. Seam 6-loop side using the ch 3, 1sc method. Ease into palm opening and sew to WS glove allowing a small overlap at thumb base. Turn RS out. Rep for 2nd thumb.

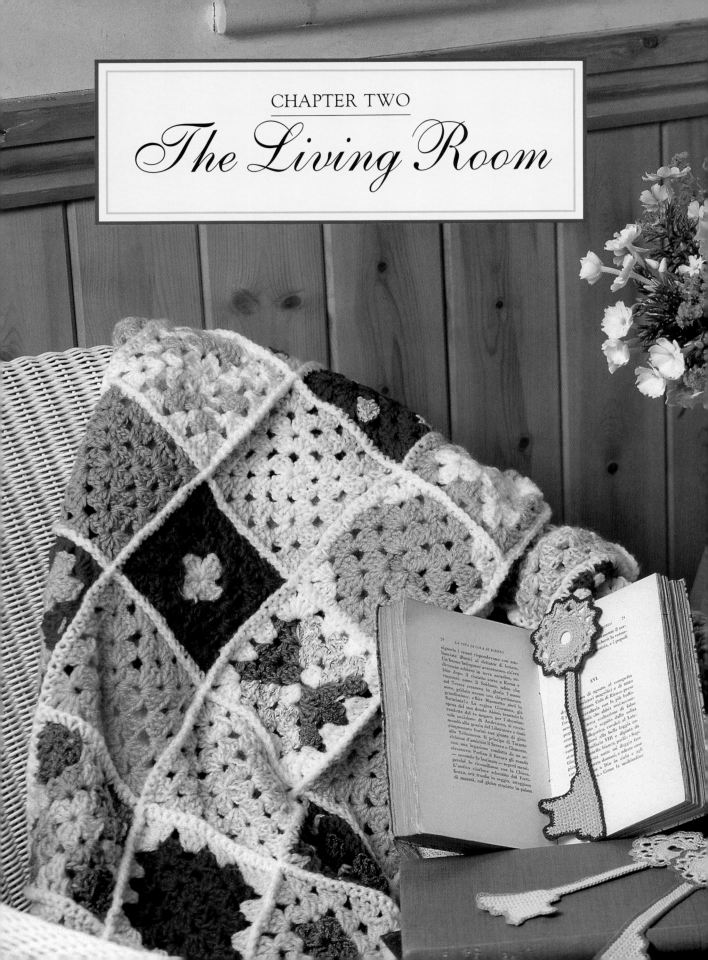

CHAPTER TWO
The Living Room

ON THE CHAIR: *Sofa Throw (page 33)*; *Key Bookmarks (page 30)*; ON THE TABLE: *Lamp Shade (page 31)*; *Playing Cards Envelope (page 32)*; *Picture Frame (page 35)*, and the *Doily (page 42)* shown in two colors.

KEY BOOKMARK

❋

This unusual bookmark design, worked in contrasting fine cottons, makes an ideal small gift or stocking filler for the bookworm in the family.

◆

MATERIALS

1oz (20g) Twilleys 20 Crochet Cotton
Small amount contrasting color (CC) for edging
Size 7 steel (1.50mm) hook
Sewing needle

◆

GAUGE

35sc = 4 inches (10cm)

◆

LENGTH

6½ inches (17cm)

◆

BASE AND STEM

Ch 53.
Row 1: 1sc into 2nd ch from hook, 1sc into each foll ch to end, turn.
Row 2: Ch 1 (1st sc), 1sc into each foll st to end, turn. (52sts.)
Rep last row once more.
Row 4: Ch 1 (1st sc), 1sc into each of next 17sts, turn.

Row 5: Ch 1 (1st sc), 1sc into each of next 15sts, turn.
Rows 6–7: Rep last row twice more. (16sts.)
Row 8: Ch 1, 1sl st into each of 2nd and 3rd sts, ch 1 (1st sc), 1sc into each of next 10sts, turn. (11sts.)
Row 9: Ch 1 (1st sc), 1sc into each of next 10sts, turn.
Rows 10–15: Rep last row 6 times more.
Row 16: Ch 1 (1st sc), 1sc into each of next 2sts, turn.
Rep last row twice more. Break yarn and fasten off. Do not turn. Rejoin yarn to 3rd sc from opp end and work ch 1 (1st sc), 1sc into each of next 2sts, turn. Rep last row twice more.
Break yarn and fasten off.

◆

TOP

(See below.)
Ch 15. Join with sl st into circle.
Round 1: Ch 1, 30sc into circle, sl st into 1st sc. (30sts.)
Round 2: Ch 1 (1st sc), 1sc into each foll st to end, sl st into 1st sc.
Round 3: Rep last round once more.
Round 4: Ch 1 (1st sc), 1sc into each of next 3sts, 2sc into next st, *1sc into each of next 4sts, 2sc into next st.

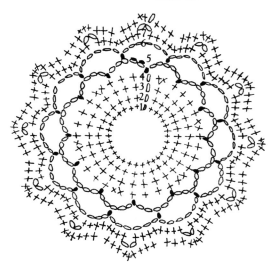

Chart for top section of the bookmark

30

Rep from * to end, sl st into 1st sc.

Round 5: *Ch 5, skip next 2sts, 1sl st into next st. Rep from * to end, working final sl st into base of 1st 5ch. (12 loops.)

Round 6: Ch 6 to center of 1st 5ch, *1sl st into next 5ch sp, ch 6.

Rep from * to end. Do not sl st.

Round 7: *Into next 6ch sp, (4sc, ch 2, 4sc).

Rep from * to end, sl st into 1st sc.

Break yarn and fasten off.

Sew stem to first few sc rounds (WS) between "petals." Sew in all rem ends.

With RS facing, join CC yarn to 2ch sp of a petal, ch 1 (1st sc), 2sc into same 2ch sp, *1sc into each of next 3sc, skip 4th sc and 1st sc of next petal, 1sc into each of next 3sc, 3sc into next 2ch sp.

Rep from * omitting last 3sc at end of round. Sl st into 1st sc. Break yarn and fasten off.

Sc evenly all around rem key edge. At inner angles work 3sc tog and at outer angles work 3sc into each corner st.

LAMP SHADE

✳

An old lamp shade can be "recalled to life" with a new crocheted cover for the frame. Choose a crochet cotton in a color that harmonizes with the lamp base and the other furnishings.

◆

MATERIALS

Size 10 crochet cotton (yarn shown: DMC Cordonnet Spécial No. 10)
(see below)
Size B/1 (2.00mm) hook
Sewing needle
All-purpose adhesive

◆

MEASUREMENTS

The lamp shade shown uses a frame measuring 7½ inches (19cm) tall with top and base dias of 4¾ inches (12cm) and 10 inches (25cm), respectively, and requires a total of about 430 yards (395m) of yarn.

◆

INSTRUCTIONS

Make a length of ch to fit fairly tightly around top of frame. Join with sl st into circle, and work 3 rounds of sc without sl st.

Round 4: 1hdc into next st, 1dc into each foll st to end.

Continue until approx ½ inch (1cm) from frame base by working 1dc into each sp formed between sts. Fit crochet over frame frequently, and inc dcs very gradually and as necessary to keep fabric close to frame.

End last round with 1hdc into each of next 3 sps. Sc 4 more rounds, working 1sc into each sp for the 1st round. End with 1sl st. Break yarn and fasten off. Sew in ends.

Fit onto frame. Fold sc rounds over top and base to inside. Sew down using the same yarn for strength. Dampen, and allow to dry.

◆

TRIMMING

(To obtain exact length required more easily, each row can be worked from the same end, and therefore quickly unraveled, or work as usual and overlap or butt ends, snipping and unpicking if necessary.) Make an even no. of ch to fit adequately around frame base.

Row 1: 1sc into 2nd ch from hook, 1sc into each foll ch to end, turn.

Row 2: Ch 1 (1st sc), 1sc into each foll st to end, turn.

Row 3: As Row 2, but a little tighter, turn.

Row 4: *Ch 3, skip next st, 1sl st into next st. Rep from * to end, turn.

Row 5: Ch 1, (2sc, ch 2, 2sc) into each loop to end. Break yarn and fasten off.

Glue to outside of base.

Make a second length of trimming, and glue to outside of top.

PLAYING CARDS ENVELOPE

✳✳

Cunningly worked in a single piece, then folded and sewn into shape, this is the perfect gift for bridge and other cards enthusiasts.

◆

MATERIALS

Small skein/ball of a size 3 firmly twisted crochet cotton (yarn shown: Twilleys Secco No. 3 Cotton)
Small amount 2nd color—optional
Size E/4 (3.50mm) hook
Matching sewing thread and needle
Large snap fastener
Button or bead

◆

GAUGE

20sc = 4 inches (10cm) across, over patt

◆

INSTRUCTIONS

Ch 37.

Row 1: (RS) 1sc into 2nd ch from hook, 1sc into each foll ch to end, turn.

Row 2: Ch 1 (1st st), 1sc into each foll st to end, turn.

Row 3: Ch 1 (1st st), *skip next st, 2sc into foll st. Rep from * to last st, 1sc, turn. (36sts.)

Rep last row until work measures approx 2½ inches (6.5cm) from base.

Next row: 1sl st into 1st st and each of next 6sts. Ch 1 for 1st sc. Mark this st. (Skip next st, 2sc into foll st) 11 times, 1sc into next st, turn.

Next row: Ch 1 (1st st), *skip next st, 2sc into foll st. Rep from * to last st (marked st), 1sc, turn.

Cont patt on these 24sts until 10 inches (25cm) from base. Break yarn and fasten off leaving a 16-inch (40cm) end for sewing.

Bring down both ends of last row to WS center to form a point (see above right) and sew edges (each half of last row) together. Catch down opening with a few loose sts. With WS still facing, fold forward side A level with C. Turn work over. Starting at point E, with 2nd col if used, insert

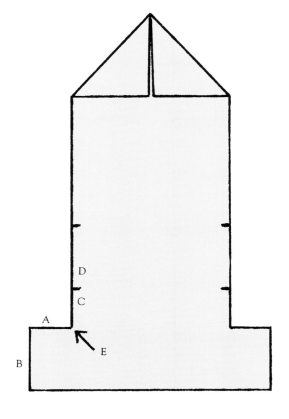

Diagram of envelope, showing positions of folds

hook, ch 1 for 1st st, and join A and C together with 6 more sc.

Bring side B level with D and join together with 11sc. Cont sc evenly along remainder of side to doubled fabric. Inc 1sc, and sc through both thicknesses of folded edge to point. Work 3sc here. Work back similarly along rem side, matching 1st side.

Pinch fabric down side of front pocket and work 11sc through two thicknesses to top opening. Rep on opposite side of pocket. At top center of pocket sides, sew a very small tuck (RS together). Sew on snap to close envelope, and cover on RS with a pretty button or bead.

SOFA THROW

❋

Yarn from old sweaters can be recycled to make a wide range of attractive crochet items by combining these Granny squares in different ways.

◆
MATERIALS

Knitting worsted yarn (approx 8,500 yards [7,070m] is sufficient for a throw measuring 6 x 9 feet [183 x 275cm])
Size F/5 or G/6 (4.00 or 4.50mm) hook
Tapestry needle

◆
INSTRUCTIONS

If reusing yarn, wind it into skeins around the arms or back of a chair. Remove, and hold tautly (and very carefully) over a boiling kettle spout to flatten the wrinkles.

Instead of working a round or rounds in one color, make more interesting patterns by varying colors of the 3dc forming each cluster. When changing color, work the final (3rd) stage of a dc stitch with the next color to be used, and twist colors on WS every few stitches as the work progresses.

Join completed squares with sc on RS using one color only, and finish with a border of one or more rounds of sc.

To reduce the number of ends to be darned in, the pattern below uses 3sl st to take a color to the first cluster of a new round.

◆
INDIVIDUAL SQUARES

Ch 4. Join with sl st into circle.

Round 1: Ch 3 (1st dc), 2dc into circle, ch 2, (3dc into circle, ch 2) 3 times, sl st into top of 3ch. Work sl st into each of next 2sts, 1sl st into next sp.

Round 2: Ch 3 (1st dc), (2dc, ch 2, 3dc) into same sp, *ch 1, (3dc, ch 2, 3dc) into next sp. Rep from * twice more, ch 1, sl st into top of 3ch, 2sl st, 1sl st into next sp.

Round 3: Ch 3 (1st dc), (2dc, ch 3, 3dc) into same corner sp, *ch 1, 3dc into next side sp, ch 1, (3dc, ch 2, 3dc) into next corner sp.

Round 4: Ch 3 (1st dc), (2dc, ch 2, 3dc) into same corner sp, *(ch 1, 3dc into next side sp) twice, ch 1, (3dc, ch 2, 3dc) into next sp. Rep from * twice more, ch 1 (3dc into next sp, ch 1) twice, sl st into top of 3ch.

ANTIMACASSAR

❋ ❋

Matching crocheted circles in three sizes are placed in such a way as to make a very pretty edging to this chair-back cover.

◆
MATERIALS

400 yards (370m) of a size 20 crochet cotton (yarn shown: DMC Cebelia No. 20)
Size 7 steel (1.50mm) hook
Piece of linen or linen-blend fabric 17 × 25 inches (44 × 63cm) without selvage

Matching sewing thread
Sewing needle
Embroidery needle

◆
GAUGE

Work to complete circles 1, 2, and 3 to equal 3¾, 3¼, and 2 inches (9.5, 8, and 5.75cm), respectively

◆
OVERALL MEASUREMENTS

29 × 16 inches (74 × 40cm)

INDIVIDUAL CIRCLES

Circle 1: approx 3¾-inch (9.5cm) dia. Make 5.
Ch 4. Join with sl st into circle.

Round 1: Ch 4 (1st tr), 1tr into circle, ch 3, (2tr into circle, ch 3) 5 times, sl st into top of 4ch.

Round 2: Sl st between 1st 2tr, ch 4 (1st tr), (1tr, ch 2, 2tr) into same sp, ch 3, skip next 3ch, *(2tr, ch 2, 2tr) into next tr pair, ch 3, skip next 3ch. Rep from * to end, sl st into top of 4ch.

Round 3: Sl st between 1st 2tr, ch 4 (1st tr), 1tr into same sp, ch 4, skip next 2ch, *2tr into next tr pair, ch 4, skip next 2ch/3ch.
Rep from * to end, sl st into top of 1st 4ch. (12tr pairs.)

Round 4: Sl st between 1st 2dr, ch 4 (1st tr), (1tr, ch 3, 2 tr) into same sp, ch 3, skip next 4ch, *(2tr, ch 3, 2tr) into next tr pair, ch 3, skip next 4ch. Rep from * to end, sl st into top of 4ch.

Round 5: Sl st between 1st 2tr, ch 3 (1st dc), 1dc into same sp, 2hdc into next 3ch sp. 2dc into next tr pair, 3dc into next 3ch sp, *2dc into next tr pair, 2hdc into next 3ch sp, 2dc into next tr pair, 3dc into next 3ch sp.
Rep from * to end, sl st into top of 1st 3ch. (108sts.)

Round 6: Ch 1 (1st sc). Work 1sc into each foll st to end, sl st into 1st sc.

Round 7: *Ch 4, skip next 2sc, 1sl st into next sc. Rep from * to end, working last sl st into 1st 4ch base.

Round 8: 2sl st along 1st ch loop, 1sl st into 1st ch loop sp, *ch 5, 1sl st into next ch loop sp. Rep from * to end, working last sl st into 1st 5ch base. Break yarn and fasten off. Sew in ends.

Circle 2: approx 3¼-inch (8cm) dia. Make 2.
Rounds 1–3: Work as for Circle 1.
Round 4: Sl st between 1st 2tr, ch 3 (1st dc), 1dc into same sp, 5hdc into next 4ch sp, *2dc into next tr pair, 5hdc into next 4ch sp.
Rep from * to end, sl st into top of 3ch. (84sts.)
Rep Rnds 6, 7, and 8 of Circle 1.
Break yarn and fasten off. Sew in ends.

Circle 2: approx 2-inch (5.7cm) dia. Make 7.
Rounds 1 and 2: Work as for Circle 1.
Round 3: Sl st between 1st 2tr, ch 3 (1st dc), 1dc into same sp, 2hdc into next 2ch sp, 2dc into next

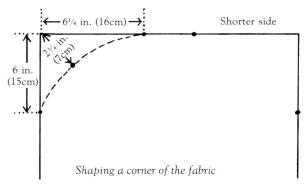

Shaping a corner of the fabric

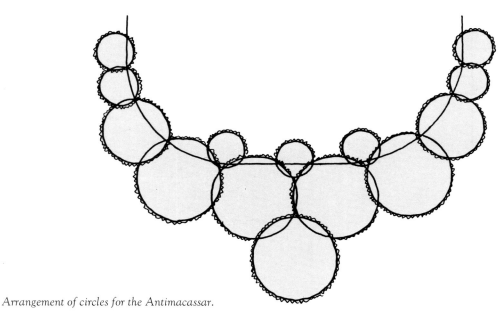

Arrangement of circles for the Antimacassar.

tr pair, 3hdc into next 3ch sp, *2dc into next tr pair, 2hdc into next 2ch sp, 2dc into next tr pair, 3hdc into next 3ch sp.
Rep from * to end, sl st into top of 3ch. (54 sts.)
Rep Rnds 6, 7, and 8 of Circle 1.
Break yarn and fasten off. Sew in ends.

SHAPING END OF FABRIC

From one corner make a mark at 6 inches (15cm) on one longer side, and 6¼ inches (16cm) on shorter side (see page 34, top). Diagonally and centrally from corner, mark 2¾ inches (7cm). Cut a gentle curve along the 3 marks. Cut 2nd corner at same end to match. Make a ½-inch (1cm) hem all around fabric edge.

ASSEMBLING CIRCLES

Arrange circles as in diagram, or as desired, and sew together where they overlap each other (see page 34, below). Sew down the edges that lie on the fabric, and invisibly along hemline.
With RS facing and with end circle on rhs, edge remainder of cover with 4ch loops (1sc between) equal in size to those on 7th rnd of circle. Insert hook through fabric, close to fold. At end, change to 5ch (1dc between), and incorporate outside edge only of circles.
Embroider chain st with same crochet cotton at ⅓ inch (7mm) from edge, around 3 straight sides.

PICTURE FRAME

❊❊❊

A lacy, antique frame—just what's needed to set off a very special picture.

MATERIALS

123 yards (109m) of a size 10 crochet cotton
(yarn shown: DMC Cordonnet Spécial No. 10)
Size 4 steel (1.75mm) hook
To mount, you will need:
2 pieces cardboard: 8 × 9½ inches (20 × 24cm)
10-inch (25cm-) sq piece of fabric, suitable for covering front of frame
Scrap of lining fabric
Medium iron-on interfacing (optional)
All-purpose adhesive
Spray adhesive for crochet reverse only
Scissors
Craft knife
Short piece of narrow ribbon for hanging

MEASUREMENTS

Approx (outer) 7½ × 6¼ inches (19 × 16cm)
(inner) 5¼ × 4 inches (13 × 10cm)

INSTRUCTIONS

With crochet cotton and hook, ch 184. Join with sl st into untwisted circle.
Round 1: Ch 1 (1st sc), 1sc into each of next 37ch, 3sc into next ch (for corner), 1sc into each of next 51ch, 3sc into next ch, 1sc into each of next 39ch, 3sc into next ch, 1sc into each of next 51ch, 3sc into next ch, 1sc into next ch, sl st into 1st sc.
Round 2: Ch 1 (1st sc), *skip next 2sc, (5dc into next sc, skip next 2sc, 1sc into next sc, skip next 2sc) to next corner, 9dc into corner st, skip next 2sc, 1sc into next sc.
Rep from * omitting last sc at end of round, sl st into 1st sc.
Round 3: Sl st to 3rd of 1st 5dc, ch 6, *(1sc into 3rd of next 5dc grp, ch 5) to next 9dc corner, (1sc into 3rd of 9dc, ch 11, 1sc into 7th of 9dc, ch 5) into corner.
Rep from * to end, sl st into 1st of 6ch.
Round 4: Ch 7, 1hdc into next sc, *5dc into 3rd of next 5ch, 1hdc into next sc, (ch 5, 1hdc into next sc, 5dc into 3rd of next 5ch, 1hdc into next sc) to next 11ch corner, 5dc into 3rd ch. Into 6th ch, work (1sl st, ch 3, 1sl st), 5dc into 9th ch, 1hdc into next sc.
Rep from * to last 5ch, 5dc into 3rd of 5ch, sl st into 2nd of 7ch.
Round 5: Ch 3, *1dc into next hdc, work a picot (= ch 2, 1sc into last dc made), (1dc, picot) into each of next 5dc, 1dc into next hdc.
Rep from * to next (5dc, ch 3, 5 dc) corner, skip 1st 5dc.
Into 3ch sp, work (1dtr, picot) 9 times and 1dtr once, skip 2nd 5dc grp.

Rep from * until all 4 corners are worked, 1dc into next hdc, picot, (1dc, picot) into each of next 5dc, sl st into 3rd of 1st 3ch.

Break yarn and fasten off. Sew in ends.

◆

ASSEMBLING

1 Lay crochet frame on one piece of cardboard, and cut out a rectangle approx ¼ inch (5mm) larger all around than widest parts of the crochet. Cut out another rectangle the same size from the other piece of cardboard.

2 Lay crochet on one piece of cardboard (front). Draw and cut out a window from the center of the cardboard ⅛ inch (3mm) smaller all around than inner measurement of frame.

3 From cardboard scraps, cut 3½-inch- (1cm-) wide strips for spacers, 2 to fit down each side and 1 to sit in between them along base edge of frame. Glue spacers to outer edge on WS of front piece.

4 To cover front of frame, position front piece RS down on WS main fabric. Leaving approx ¾ inch (2cm) margin all around outer edge of fabric (for folding to WS), cut out rectangle. Iron interfacing, if used, to WS of fabric.

5 Cut off a triangle from each fabric corner, approx ½ inch (1cm) from cardboard corners. Fold and glue all edges of fabric to WS of cardboard, covering spacers. Allow to dry.

6 Make a window in the fabric by cutting a rectangle ¾ inch (2cm) smaller all around than inner edges of frame.

Diagonally snip corners of fabric window into corners of carboard window. Fold excess fabric to WS of carboard, and glue down.

Apply additional glue to any fraying edges.

7 To help the picture slide in more easily, cut a picture frame from lining fabric approx ¼ inch (5mm) smaller than frame, and glue on WS of front.

8 On back of frame, make a tiny slit 1¼ inch (3cm) from center top. Fold and insert a small ribbon loop for hanging.

Glue ends to WS.

9 Apply glue along edges only to base and sides of WS back, and affix to front.

10 Using spray adhesive, attach crochet frame to fabric. Insert photograph.

"Windows" Pillow (page 38); Antimacassar (page 33); Afghan (page 38).

AFGHAN

❀

Useful on wintry evenings, this checker-board afghan is perfect for tucking over knees while playing cards or relaxing before bed.

♦

MATERIALS

660 yards (600m) of a knitting worsted in each of colors A and B (yarn shown: Jarol Supersaver Double Knitting)
Size J/10 (6.00mm) hook
Tapestry needle

♦

GAUGE

16sc and 20 rows = 4¼ inches (11cm) sq

♦

MEASUREMENTS

Approx 30 × 41 inches (77 × 105cm)

♦

INSTRUCTIONS

The blanket is worked in strips of single crochet, sewn together.
With col A ch 17

Row 1: 1sc into 2nd ch from hook, 1sc into each foll ch to end, turn.
Row 2: Ch 1 (1st sc), 1sc into each foll st to end, turn. (16sts.)
Form a square by repeating last row 18 times more. Change to next color when working the sc at end of final row by drawing through new color to start next row.
Work 20 rows with col B.
Cont alternating colors every 20 rows until the work is 9 sqs in length. Start next strip with col B and so on, so that a pattern of checks is formed with 7 strips.
Place the flat of 2 strips together, matching rows. Overcast along edge. When all strips are joined, work 4ch loops with either color yarn along each shorter edge—5 loops across each square. Sew in ends.
Make a fring by knotting 4 × 8 inch- (20cm-) long strands of yarn into each loop. Use col A next to a col B square, and col B next to a col A square.

"WINDOWS" PILLOW

❀❀

The "window" panels worked on the front of this cushion could be backed with the same fabric as that used for draperies or other furnishings, or with a harmonizing fabric, to create a sophisticated designer look.

♦

MATERIALS

4,350 yards (4,000m) of a size 3 firmly twisted crochet cotton (yarn shown: Twilleys Secco No. 3 Cotton)
Size E/4 (3.50mm) hook
13½-inch (35cm-) sq furnishing fabric
Approx 13½-inch (35cm-) sq pillow form
Matching sewing thread and needle
Velcro or zipper (optional)

♦

GAUGE

20sc and 20 rows = 4 inches (10cm) sq

♦

FRONT

Ch 78.
Row 1: (RS) 1sc into 2nd ch from hook, 1sc into each foll ch to end, turn.
Row 2: Ch 2 (1st st), 1sc into front top loop of next (2nd) st, *1sc into back loop of next st, 1sc into front top loop of next st.
Rep from * to last st, 1sc into both loops, turn. (77sts.)
Rep last row until 2¼ inches (6cm) have been worked, ending with RS facing for next row.

RIGHT-HAND BORDER

Ch 2 (1st st). Retaining patt, work 1sc into each of next 11sts, 1sc (both loops) into next st, turn.
Rep last row until approx 6¼ inches (16cm) from base ch, ending at inside edge. Break yarn and fasten off.

VERTICAL BAR OF CROSS

With RS facing, rejoin yarn to 23rd st from 13sts of RH border (i.e., 36th st from rhs). Ch 2 (1st st). Retaining patt, but working 1sc into back top loop for the 2nd st of each row, work 1sc into each of next 6sts. Cont patt on these 7sts until vertical bar of cross equals length of RH border.
End at lhs with RS facing. Break yarn and fasten off.

LEFT-HAND BORDER

With RS still facing, rejoin yarn to 13th st from lhs. Ch 2 (1st st).
Retaining patt (as Row 2 of front), work to end, turn.
Cont patt of these 13sts until LH border equals length of RH border.
End at outside edge. Turn.

HORIZONTAL BAR OF CROSS

Next row: Ch 2 (1st st), patt next 12sts, ch 22, 1sc into front top loop of 1st of 7 center sts, 1sc into back top loop of next st. Patt next 5sts, ch 22, 1sc into back top loop of 1st of 13 RH border sts, patt to end, turn.
Next row: Ch 2 (1st st), patt to 1st 22ch, 1sc into each ch st, 1sc into front top loop of 1st of 7 center sts, patt next 6sts, 1sc into each of next 22ch, 1sc into back top loop of 1st of next 13sts, patt to end. (77 sts)**.
Rep Row 2 of front until length of horizontal bar and width of vertical bar of cross are fairly equal, and ending with RS facing for next row.
Work RH and LH borders, and vertical bar of cross, as before, so that 4 fairly square "windows" will be formed.
Rep from ** to ** once more.
Cont until lengths of both top and bottom borders are equal. Break yarn and fasten off.

BACK

Work as for front until end of Row 2.

Rep Row 2 until lengths of back and front are equal. Break yarn and fasten off.
With RS of front facing, work 21sc—or adjust as necessary—along vertical sides of each window. Sew in all ends.

PANEL

Ch 79.
Row 1: 1tr into 11th ch from hook, *ch 3, skip next 3ch, 1 tr into next ch. Rep from * to end, turn. (18sqs.)
Work to a gauge of 7 × 7sqs = window opening.
Row 2: Ch 7 (tr + 3ch), 1tr into next tr, *ch 3, skip next 3ch, 1tr into next tr.
Rep from * to end, turn.
Rep last row until 18sqs in length.
Break yarn and fasten off.
Sew panel behind front openings, concealing 2 lines of sqs behind vertical and horizontal bars of cross—attach edge trs just behind window edges.
Sew outer edges of panel to WS of front.

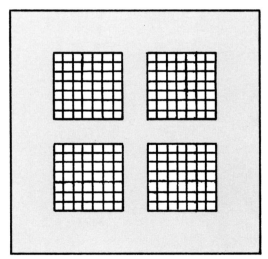

Completed pillow front, showing four "windows"

Trim fabric ¾ inch (2cm) larger all around than 18sq panel, rounding off corners. Overcast edge to prevent fraying. Turn under ⅜ inch (1cm) all around onto RS, center RS of fabric against WS of panel, and sew down edge.
On RS, join pillow back and front along 3 sides with even sc, increasing as necessary at corners—leave base ch side open.
Insert pillow form, loosely overcast open edges together, or insert zipper or Velcro fastening.

NEEDLECASE WITH PICOT CROCHET EDGE

✳✳

The arch shape was chosen to hold sewing needles of differing lengths. When designing the embroidery, adapt the shape to represent a tunnel, window, or whatever takes your fancy, to create a personalized needlecase for yourself or to give as a gift.

MATERIALS

5 × 2¼ inch (13 × 8cm) piece of linen or any suitable plain fabric
Lightweight lining fabric
Iron-on interfacing
Scrap of felt to hold needles
6-strand embroidery floss in 2 or more colors
Size 4 steel (1.75mm) hook
Matching sewing thread
Sewing needle
Crewel needle

INSTRUCTIONS

1 Cut out both fabrics and interfacing following the pattern on page 42.

2 Cut the interfacing into 3 pieces—2 arches and spine. Trim so that arched pieces are ¼ inch (5mm) smaller around than fabric (each arch will be 2 inches [5cm] wide). The narrow ¼-inch (5mm) strip remaining is for the "spine," as on book cover.

3 Place RS of main fabric and lining together, baste, and stitch edges, excluding base, with ¼ inch (5mm) seam allowance.

4 Trim around stitched edges and clip curves. Turn RS out and press.

5 Work embroidery on the front, using one or two strands of floss. Work through main fabric only.

6 Iron the 3 pieces of interfacing to WS of main fabric, trimming the interfacing if necessary.

RIGHT: *Place Mat (page 42).*

40

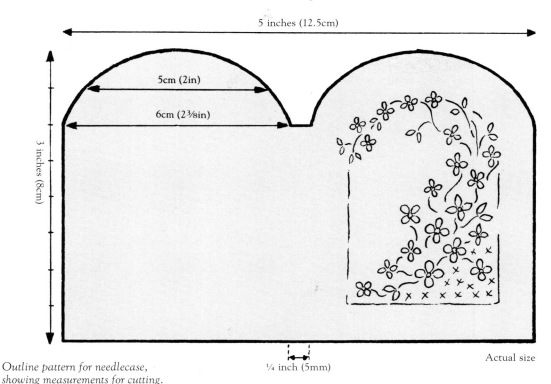

Outline pattern for needlecase, showing measurements for cutting.

5 inches (12.5cm)

3 inches (8cm)

5cm (2in)

6cm (2⅜in)

¼ inch (5mm)

Actual size

7 Turn RS out. Turn in base edges ¼ inch (5mm) and sew by hand. Using two strands of floss and working 3–4sts to ⅜ inch (1cm), back-stitch close to edge all around RS of needlecase. Back-stitch two parallel lines ¼ inch (5mm) apart for spine, through both fabrics. The sts should not be too tight, to allow for insertion of crochet hook.

◆

EDGING

Row 1: Using same color and thickness of floss as back stitch and with RS facing, work 1sc into each st. Inc as necessary at corners. Sl st at end. Break off first color.

Row 2: Omit spine. Using second color, ch 3, 1sc into 3rd ch from hook, 1sc into next st. Rep from * to end, 1sl st.

Break yarn and fasten off. Sew in ends. Press. Attach arch-shaped felt "pages" by making a line of stitches down center spine, inserting needle through felt, lining, and back only of main fabric.

DOILY
✳✳✳

Worked in fine cotton, this lacy doily is edged with a narrow border of coronets and would add a touch of formality to any occasion.

◆

MATERIALS

440 yards (405m) of a size 20 crochet cotton (yarn shown: Coats Crochet Cotton No. 20) Size 8 steel (1.25mm) hook

◆

MEASUREMENTS

Approx 13½ inches (34cm) dia

◆

INSTRUCTIONS

Ch 5. Join with sl st into circle.

Round 1: Ch 6, (1tr, ch 2) 11 times into circle, sl st into 4th of 6ch.

Round 2: Sl st into 1st 2ch sp, ch 10, 1dc into same sp, *(1dc, ch 7, 1dc) into next sp.

Rep from * to end, sl st into 3rd of 10ch. (12 loops.)

Round 3: Ch 4 (1st tr), sl st into 4th of rem 7ch, 1tr into next dc, ch 7, *1tr into next dc, sl st into 4th of next 7ch, 1tr into next dc, ch 7.

Rep from * to end, sl st into top of 4ch.

Round 4: Ch 11, skip 1st center sl st, 1tr into 2nd tr of last round, sl st into 4th of next 7ch, *1tr into next center sl st, ch 7, 1tr into next tr, sl st into 4th of next 7ch.

Rep from * to end, sl st into 4th of 11ch.

Round 5: Ch 2 (1st hdc), *1sc into each of next 3ch, ch 1, skip 1ch, 1sc into each of next 3ch sts, 1hdc into next sl st, ch 2, 1hdc into next tr.

Rep from * to end, omitting last hdc at end of round, sl st into top of 1st 2ch.

Round 6: *Ch 7, 1sc into next 1ch sp, ch 7, 1sc into next 2ch sp.

Rep from * to end.

Round 7: 2sl st into 1st 7ch sp, ch 4 (1st tr), (1tr, ch 7, 2tr) into same sp, *(2tr, ch7, 2tr) into next 7ch sp.

Rep from * to end, sl st into top of 4ch.

Round 8: Ch 4 (1st tr), 1tr into next tr, *sl st into 4th of next 7ch, 1 tr into each of next 2tr, ch 7, 1tr into each of next 2tr.

Rep from * to end, omitting last 2tr at end of round, sl st into top of 4ch.

Round 9: Sl st into next (2nd) tr, ch 4 (1st tr), 1tr into next sl st, *ch 7, 1tr into each of next 2tr, sl st into 4th of next 7ch, skip next tr, 1tr into next tr, 1tr into next sl st.

Rep from * to end, omitting last 2tr at end of round, sl st into top of 4ch.

Round 10: Ch 4 (1st tr), 1tr into next tr, sl st into 4th of next 7ch. Cont patt set in last round. End with ch 7, sl st into top of 4ch.

Round 11: As Rnd 9.

Round 12: Ch 2 (1st hdc), 1hdc into next tr, *1sc into each of next 3 ch, ch 2, skip 1 ch, 1sc into each of next 3ch, skip next 1tr, 1hdc into each of next tr and sl st, ch 4, 1hdc into each of next 2tr.

Rep from * to end, omitting last 2hdc at end of round, sl st into top of 1st 2ch.

Round 13: 1sl st back into prev 4ch sp, *ch 7, 1sc into next 2ch sp, ch 7, 1sc into next 4ch sp.

Rep from * to end, working the last dc into same sp as sl st.

Rounds 14–16: As Rnds 7–9.

Pattern sketch of a section of the doily

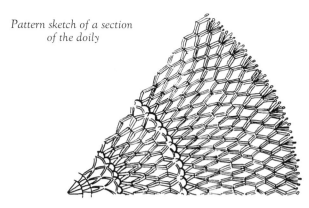

Rounds 17–20: Cont patt set in Rnd 9 for 4 more rounds.

Round 21: As patt but increase the 7ch to 9ch.

Round 22: Cont with 9ch and patt but work dtr instead of tr, and sl st into 5th of 9ch (5ch for 1st dtr).

Round 23: (Start from 1st dtr at left of center sl st) ch 6, 2dtr into st at 6ch base, (ch 6, 1 sl st into 4th ch from hook, ch 2 = picot), *2dtr into next dtr, sl st into 5th of next 9ch, ch 4, 1sl st into same 5th of 9ch, 2dtr into next dtr, picot, (2dtr, 1ttr) into next dtr, picot, skip sl st, "(1ttr, 2dtr) into next dtr, picot."

Rep from * to end, omitting from "to" at end of round, sl st into top of 1st 6ch.

Ease sts of Rnds 7 and 14 to center of each 7ch loop.

PLACE MAT

For a place mat (approx 10 inches [25cm] dia), work exactly as for Doily, but with changes to the following rounds. (Uses 175 yards [160m] cotton.)

To start, ch 4 (instead of 5) to make a circle. Substitute Rnd 1a (below) for Rnd 1.

Round 1a: Ch 5, (1dc, ch 2) 11 times into circle, sl st into 3rd of 5ch.

Add Rnd 4a (below) between Rnds 4 and 5.

Round 4a: Ch 4 (1st tr), sl st into 4th of rem 7ch, 1tr into next center sl st, ch 8, *1tr into next tr, sl st into 4th of next 7ch, 1tr into next center sl st, ch 8. Rep from * to end, sl st into top of 4ch (2nd col, if required), sl st into next tr.

Round 5: Into the 8ch, work (4sc, ch 1, 4sc).

Round 6: (1st col) Make 5ch and not 7ch loops.

Round 7: Work into 5ch and not 7ch sps.

Omit Rnds 11–20 incl.

Round 22: Work this rnd 3 times (instead of once).

Round 23: As Doily.

Ice Cream Cone Border (page 46); Beaded Pitcher Cover (page 51); Coffee Jar Covers (page 47); Egg Cozies (page 48).

CHAPTER THREE

The Kitchen

ICE CREAM CONE BORDER

✳✳

A fun addition to the kitchen, these crocheted "cones," with their cotton "ice cream," will stimulate the appetite of children and adults alike!

MATERIALS

270 yards (247m) of a matte-finish sport-weight cotton (yarn shown: Twilleys No. 1 Handicraft Cotton)
Size F/5 (4.00mm) hook
Scissors
Cotton fabric for ice-cream appliqué
Matching sewing thread and needle
Medium iron-on interfacing
Thin cardboard

GAUGE

3 inches (8cm) across top × 6 inches (15cm) long = 1 point (cone)

MEASUREMENTS

42 × 8½ inches (107 × 22cm) = 10 points joined and completed

POINTS

Ch 4.
Row 1: Skip 3ch, 1dc into 4th ch from hook, turn. (1st 3ch count as 1st dc.)
Row 2: Ch 3, 1dc into 1st st (top of dc of 1st row), 1dc into top of 3ch, turn. (3sts.)
Row 3: Ch 3, 1dc into 1st st, 1dc into each of next 2sts, turn. (4sts.)
Row 4: Ch 3, 1dc into 1st st, 1dc into each of next 3sts, turn. (5sts.)
Cont inc of 1dc at beg of each row until 12 sts. Break yarn and fasten off.
Make 10 or as many points as required. Do not break yarn at end of last point. Turn.

HEADING

Row 1: Join points together as follows: ch 3, 1dc into 1st st, 1dc into each of rem 11sts.
Inc at start of each point as before, work 13dc across each rem point, (slip-knot ends at rhs), turn.
Rows 2–6: Ch 3, 1dc into next and each foll st to end, turn.

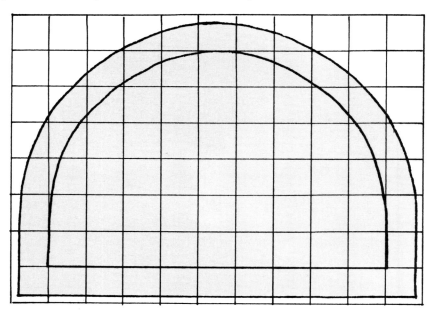

Patterns for small and large semicircles (actual size) for interfacing and fabric

Actual size

Row 7: Ch 2, 1sc into 2nd st, *ch 1, 1sc into next st. Rep from * to end.

Break yarn and fasten off. Sew in ends.

Use diagram on page 46 to cut out the two semicircles from cardboard and use as templates. For each point, cut out the smaller semicircle from interfacing and larger semicircle from fabric.

Fuse interfacing to fabric.

Turn in raw edges of fabric, baste, and appliqué onto crochet (see right).

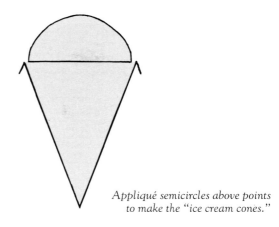

Appliqué semicircles above points to make the "ice cream cones."

COFFEE JAR COVER

Instead of throwing away an empty coffee jar, transform it into a decorative and useful container by making this string mesh cover and hinged lid.

MATERIALS
Approx 55 yards (50m) thin cotton string
Size H/8 (5.00mm) hook
Large tapestry needle
All-purpose adhesive

GAUGE
14½dc = 4 inches (10cm);
1st 2 rounds = 2¾ inches (7cm) dia

MEASUREMENTS
To fit (approx) 6½ inch- (16cm-) tall × 8 inch- (20cm-) circumference jar

COVER
Ch 5. Join with sl st into circle.

Round 1: Ch 3 (1st dc), 14dc into circle, sl st into top of 2ch.

Round 2: Ch 3, 1dc into same place as 3ch, *2dc into next dc.
Rep from * to end, sl st into top of 3ch.

Rounds 3–5: Ch 1 (1st sc), 1sc into each foll st to end, sl st into 1st sc.

Round 6: Ch 2, skip next sc, 1sc into next sc. Rep from * working last sc into 1st 2ch sp.

Round 7: Ch 2, *1sc into next 2ch sp, ch 2. Rep from * to end.

Place marker beneath last st and treat round ends as being vertically above marker.

Rounds 8–16: Beg with 1sc into next 2ch sp, rep last round 9 times more (or no. of times necessary for cover to reach, when fully stretched, approx 1¼ inch [3cm] from jar rim).

Round 17: Work 2sc into each foll 2ch sp to end, sl st into 1st sc.

Reinsert marker to indicate round ends.

Round 18: Ch 1 (1st sc), 1sc into each foll sc to end, sl st into 1st sc.

Rounds 19–22: Rep last round 4 times more.

Break yarn, leaving a 10-inch (25cm) end for gathering. Fasten off.

Stretch cover over jar and gather top to fit inside rim, ¾ inch (2cm) down and around. Glue inside rim. Temporarily wedge a cardboard tube or similar item inside to hold until glue is dry.

LID
Ch 140.

1sc into 2nd ch from hook, 1sc into each foll ch to end. Ch 5, turn, and make sl st into last sc made. Break yarn, leaving a 16-inch (40cm) end.

Buttonhole-stitched handle at one end of sc strip

turn handle, gluing and coiling the crochet strip tightly around handle base, ending up with a flat disk (jar-top size) with handle protruding from center. Now shape a gentle upward slope toward center (see below).

Completed shape of lid

Around the 5ch, work a tight buttonhole st (see Techniques) with the end, into 5ch sp, for the handle (see above). Secure ends in WS of sc row. Beg at same end (RS outside and right way up),

Smear a little more glue onto underside of lid, and allow to dry.
Sew 2 loose hinges between lid and cover.

EGG COZY

Give a soft-boiled egg a jaunty look—and keep it warm—with an amusing little hat. Perfect for using up extra bits of yarn.

◆

MATERIALS
Scraps of knitting worsted (2 colors)
Size F/5 (4.00mm) hook; size E/4 (3.50mm) for final round
Tapestry needle

◆

GAUGE
1st 2 rounds—1¼ inches (3cm) dia (medium cozy)
1½ inches (3.5cm) dia (large cozy)

◆

INSTRUCTIONS
With 1st col and larger hook, ch 3. Join with sl st into circle.
Round 1: Ch 2 (1st hdc), 7hdc into circle.

Use small safety pin to indicate round ends.
Round 2: 2sc into each of 8hdc.
Round 3: 1sc into each sc.
Round 4: *1sc into next sc, 2sc into foll sc. Rep from * to end. (24sts.)
Rounds 5–9: As Rnd 3.
Round 10: 1 sl st into next dc, ch 2 (1st hdc), 1hdc into each foll sc to end, sl st into top of 2ch.
Round 11: Ch 2 (1st hdc), 1hdc into same place as ch 2, 2hdc into each foll hdc to end, sl st into top of 2ch.
Round 12: Ch2 (1st hdc), 1hdc into each foll hdc to end, sl st into top of 2ch.
Round 13: Ch 1 (1st sc), 1sc into each foll st to end, sl st into 1st sc.
(Change to 2nd col and smaller hook.)
Round 14: As Rnd 13.
Embroider a round of ch st for "hat" band using tapestry needle.

SIMPLE RUG

The coarse backing fabric will make this rug more durable than you might imagine. Choose colors that harmonize with the decor of the room for which it is intended.

◆

MATERIALS

Knitting worsted: 660 yards (600m)
each of colors A, B, C; 330 yards (300m)
color D for edges and between-stitching
(yarn shown: Jarol Supersaver Double Knitting)
Size 11 (8.00mm) hook
Burlap or any suitable rug backing
Large tapestry needle

◆

MEASUREMENTS

Approx 40 × 25 inches (1m × 65cm)

◆

INSTRUCTIONS

Use 4 strands together throughout.
With col D, ch 72.
Row 1: (RS) 1dc into 4th ch from hook, 1dc into each foll ch to end. Draw through col A during last stage of final dc, turn.
Row 2: (Col A) ch 3 (1st dc), 1 dc into each foll st to end.
Rep last row once more. Draw through col B during final dc.
Cont in dc, repeating 2 rows each of cols A, B, and C in turn until approx 24 inches (62cm) from base ch. Complete 1 row with col D.
On RS, and using col D with a large tapestry needle, overcast a line of sts between stripes of cols A, B, and C, threading yarn under LH st below top loop of each dc (see below). Secure side ends by knotting loosely together. Fold ends to WS.
Attach backing.

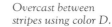

Overcast between stripes using color D.

FILET JAM JAR COVER
✳✳

A delightful gift for extra-special friends. Pop this on top of a jar of your homemade jam, and it can be used as a pretty doily once the jam is used up.

◆

MATERIALS

175 yards (160m) of a size 20 crochet cotton
(yarn shown: Twilleys 20)
Size 8 steel (1.25mm) hook

◆

GAUGE

10 × 10 sps = 2 inches (5cm) sq

MEASUREMENTS

Approx 5½ inches (14cm) dia

◆

FILET

Sp = 1dc, ch 2, 1dc. Change the 2ch to 2dc to form a block of 4dc. (Last st of sq counts as 1st st of next sq.) For further instructions on filet crochet, see p. 11.

◆

INSTRUCTIONS

Ch 24.
Row 1: 1dc into 4th ch from hook, 1dc into each of next 20ch, turn. (7 blocks.)
Row 2: Ch 8, 1dc into 4th ch from hook, 1dc into

each of next 4ch, 1dc into next dc, (ch 2, skip 2dc, 1dc into next dc) 7 times, 1tr into same place as last dc made, 1tr into base of tr. Work 1 tr into base of tr just made. Similarly, work 3 more trs to complete 2 inc blocks, turn.
Follow chart below, increasing or decreasing blocks where shown.

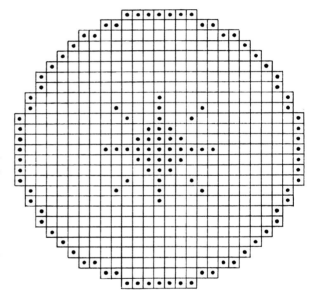

FILET SHELF EDGING
✳✳

This delicate-looking filet shelf edging would look perfect on a traditional hutch. Showing London's famous Tower Bridge, it would make a lovely souvenir of a visit to England.

◆

MATERIALS

A size 20 crochet cotton (yarn shown: DMC Cebelia No. 20 Crochet)
Size 8 steel (1.25mm) hook

◆

GAUGE

1 patt of 48 rows = 3½ × 9½ inches (9 × 24cm)

◆

MEASUREMENTS

400 yards (370m) of yarn is sufficient for approx 30 inches (75cm)

◆

FILET

Sp = 1dc, ch 2, 1dc. Change the ch 2 to 2dc to

form a block of 4dc. (Last st of sq counts as 1st st of next sq.)

For further instructions on filet crochet, see p. 11.

INSTRUCTIONS

Ch 54.

Row 1: 1dc into 4th ch from hook, 1dc into each of next 5ch, (ch 2, skip next 2ch, 1dc into next ch) 3 times, 1dc into each of next 3ch, (ch 2, skip next 2ch, 1dc into next ch) 10 times, 1dc into each of next 3ch, turn.

Follow chart below from Row 2, working block inc at beg of odd rows and block dec at end of even rows, as shown. Patt repeats after Row 48.

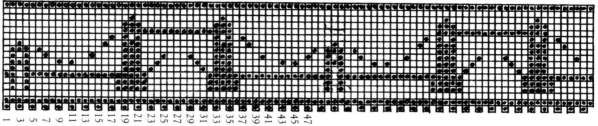

Chart for filet shelf edging (1 patt = 48 rows)

PITCHER COVER

✳ ✳ ✳

This pitcher cover, finished with beads and a muslin lining, keeps insects out of the lemonade.

MATERIALS

350 yards (320m) of a size 20 crochet cotton (yarn shown: Twilleys 20)
(2 colors)
Size 8 steel (1.25mm) hook
Approx 8 inch- (20cm-) dia circle of laundered muslin
20 beads for edge of cover. These should be fairly weighty without being too large—max ¾ inch (2cm) long
Matching sewing thread and needle

MEASUREMENTS

Approx 10 inches (25 cm) dia

INSTRUCTIONS

Ch 6. Join with sl st into circle.
Work each round using colors alternately.

Round 1: Ch 3 (1st dc), 19dc into circle, sl st into top of 3ch.

Round 2: Ch 3, 1dc into same place as 3ch, ch 2, skip next dc, *2dc into next dc, ch 2, skip next dc. Rep from * to end, sl st into top of 3ch. (10 pairs.)

Round 3: Ch 3, 1dc into same place as 3ch, ch 2, *2dc into next dc, ch 2. Rep from * to end, sl st into top of 3ch.

Round 4: Sl st into next 2ch sp, ch 3 (1st dc), (2dc, ch 2, 3dc) into same sp, ch 1, 1sc into next sp, ch 1, *(3dc, ch 2, 3dc = V grp) into next sp, ch 1, 1 sc into next sp, ch 1. Rep from * to end, sl st into top of 3ch.

Round 5: Sl st into next 2ch sp, ch 7 (dc + 4ch), 1dc into same sp, ch 3, V grp into next 2ch sp, ch 3, *(1dc, ch 4, 1dc) into next 2ch sp, ch 3, V grp into next 2ch sp, ch 3. Rep from * to end, sl st into 3rd of 7ch.

Round 6: Ch 3 (1st dc), 8dc into next 4ch sp, ch 3, V grp into next 2ch sp, ch 3, *9dc into next 4ch sp, ch 3, V grp into next 2ch sp, ch 3. Rep from * to end, sl st into top of 1st 3ch.

Round 7: Ch 3, (1sc into next dc, ch 3) 8 times, V grp into next 2ch sp, ch 3, *(1sc into next dc of 9dc grp, ch 3) 9 times, V grp into next 2ch sp, ch 3. Rep from * to end.

Round 8: *(1sc into next 3ch sp between scs, ch 3) 8 times, (V grp, ch 2, 3dc) into next 2ch sp, ch 3. Rep from * to end.

Round 9: *(1sc into next 3ch sp between scs, ch 3) 7 times, (V grp, ch 3) into each of next 2 2ch sps. Rep from * to end.

Round 10: *(1sc into next 3ch sp between scs, ch 3) 6 times, V grp into next 2ch sp, dc, (1dc, ch 4, 1dc) into next 3ch sp, ch 3, V grp into next 2ch sp, ch 3. Rep from * to end.

Round 11: *(1sc into next 3ch sp between scs, ch 3) 5 times, V grp into next 2ch sp, ch 3, 8dc into next 4ch sp, ch 3, V grp into next 2ch sp, ch 3. Rep from * to end.

Round 12: *(1sc into next 3ch sp between scs, ch 3) 4 times, V grp into next 2ch sp, ch 3, (1sc into next dc of 8dc grp, ch 3) 8 times, V grp into next 2ch sp, ch 3. Rep from * to end.

Round 13: *(1sc into next 3ch sp between scs, ch 3) 3 times, (V grp, ch 2, 3dc) into next 2ch sp, ch 3, (1sc into next 3ch sp between scs, ch 3) 7 times, (V grp, ch 2, 3dc) into next 2ch sp, ch 3.

Round 14: *(1sc into next 3ch sp between scs, ch 3) twice, (V grp, ch 3) into each of next 2 2ch sps, (1sc into next 3ch sp between scs, ch 3) 6 times, (V grp, ch 3) into each of next 2 2ch sps. Rep from * to end.

Round 15: *1sc into 3ch sp at next "pineapple" top, ch 3, V grp into next 2ch sp, ch 3, 3dc into next 3ch sp, ch 3, V grp into next 2ch sp, ch 3, (1sc into next 3ch sp between scs, ch 3) 5 times, V grp into next 2ch sp, ch 3, 3dc into next 3ch sp, ch 3, V grp into next 2ch sp, ch 3. Rep from * to end.

Round 16: Sl st into next sc stem, 6sl st to next 2ch sp, 1sl st into sp. *Ch 3 (1st dc), 2dc into same sp, ch 3, (3dc, ch 3) into each of next 2sps, V grp into next 2ch sp, ch 3, (1sc into next 3ch sp between scs, ch 3) 4 times, V grp into next 2ch sp, ch 3, (3dc, ch 3) into each of next 3sps.
Replace 1st 3ch with 1dc, and rep from * —work 1st 3dc into next 2ch sp.
Sl st into top of 1st 3ch.

RIGHT: *Filet Shelf Edging (page 50); Pitcher Cover (page 51); Filet Jam Jar Covers (page 50). Also shown are yellow gingham pitcher and jam jar covers which have crocheted picot edges (see Edgings, page 118).*
FAR RIGHT: *Pot Holders (page 54); Plant Hanger (page 55).*

Round 17: Sl st into next 3ch sp, ch 3 (1st dc), 2dc into same sp, ch 3, (3dc, ch 3) into each of next 2 sps, *V grp into next 2ch sp, ch 3, (1sc into next 3ch sp between scs, ch 3) 3 times, V grp into next 2ch sp, ch 3, (3dc, ch 3) into each of next 7 sps. Rep from * working last (3dc, ch 3) into only 4 sps at end of round, sl st into top of 1st 3ch.

Rounds 18–19: Sl st into next 3ch sp and cont patt, as set, for two more rounds.

Round 20: Sl st into next 3ch sp, ch 3 (1st dc), 2dc into same 3ch sp, ch 3. Work (3dc, ch 3) into each foll sp, skipping over (ch 3, 1sc, ch 3) above each of 5 outer pineapples.

Round 21: Cont patt, as set, to end but work V grp into next and every foll 3rd 3ch sp.
(If desired, use just one color for last 2 rounds.)

Round 22: Patt as set to end, working V grp into each 2ch sp.

Round 23: Work only 2ch between each 3dc grp, continuing with the V grp into each 2ch sp.
Break yarn and fasten off.
Center muslin circle on the WS of crochet cover and baste it in place.
Turn under edge and stitch.
Attach bead to each V grp.

POT HOLDERS

This design, used in Britain for lifting plum puddings out of boiling water, can be used for hanging potted plants. (Could also be made with suitable string.)

MATERIALS

Matte-finish sport-weight cotton (yarn shown: Twilleys No. 1 Handicraft Cotton)—small quantity
Size F/5 (4.00mm) hook

Sketch to show working of first three rounds

INSTRUCTIONS

Work first three rounds for the small basin holder (see below left), and four or five rounds for larger sizes.
Ch 14. Join with sl st into circle.

Round 1: *1 sc into circle, ch 10.
Rep from * 4 times more. Even out sts around circle. 1 sl st into start of 1st 10ch.

Round 2: Sl st to center of same ch, 1 sl st into same 10ch sp, *ch 16, 1sc into next 10ch sp.
Rep from * 3 times more, ch 16, 1sl st into start of 1st 16ch.

Round 3: Ch 21, 1sc into same (1st) 16ch sp, *ch 21, 1sc into center of sc stem at end of this ch, ch 21, 1sc into next 16ch sp.
Rep from * 3 times more, ch 21, 1sl st into start of 1st 21ch.

Round 4: Sl st to center of same ch, 1sl st into same 21ch sp, *ch 16, 1sc into next 21 ch sp.
Rep from * 8 times more, ch 16, 1sl st into start of 1st 16ch.
Rep last round once more for larger holder, working into 16ch sps.
Fasten off.

HANDLE

Make a double ch (p. 9) to an approx length of 30 inches (75cm) or 35 inches (90cm). Thread through outer loops and secure into a circle.

PLANT HANGER

The plant container is held in a honeycomb-pattern mesh between two sturdy rings covered in single crochet. The pattern is easily adapted for any size of basket.

MATERIALS

2,270 yards (2,080m) of a size 3 crochet cotton (yarn shown: Twilleys Stalite Perlespun No. 3)

2 ounces (50g) artificial raffia

Sizes F/5 and J/10 (4.00 and 6.00mm) hooks

2 strong, narrow metal rings, 2 inches (5cm) and 4 inches (10cm) dia

Tapestry needle

Lightweight basket—approx 10 inches (25cm) dia × 3½ inches (9cm) tall

INSTRUCTIONS

With size 3 yarn and smaller hook, work approx 200sc around larger ring to conceal metal, making even-sized sts and not too tight. Break yarn and fasten off. Twist sts into a spiral, approx 24 times. Sew in ends, joining circle of sts.

To make the covering for the basket, use yarn, doubled, and larger hook.

Round 1: Work 48sc around smaller ring. Sl st into 1st st.

Round 2: Ch 4 (1st dc + 1ch), skip next st, *1dc into next st, ch 1, skip next st.

Rep from * to end, sl st into 3rd of 4ch, sl st into next sp.

Round 3: Ch 5 (1st dc + 2ch), *1dc into next sp, ch 2. Rep from * to end, sl st into 3rd of 5ch, ch 1, sl st into next sp.

Round 4: Ch 6 (1st dc + 3ch), *1dc into next sp, ch 3. Rep from * to end, sl st into 3rd of 6ch, ch2, sl st into next sp.

Rounds 5 and 6: Ch 7 (1st dc + 4ch), *1dc into next sp, ch 4.

Rep from * to end, skip 2ch, sl st into 3rd of 7ch, ch 2, sl st into next sp.

Rounds 7 and 8: Ch 8 (1st dc + 5ch), *1dc into next sp, ch 5.

Rep from * to end, skip 2ch, sl st into 3rd of 8ch. Fasten off and sew in ends.

For the "strings," use the same hook and doubled yarn, and make a double ch, a little over 4½ yards (4.3m) in length. Leaving 8 inches (20cm) for sewing ends together, break yarn and fasten off. Weave string through outer loops of cover, and 4 times through larger ring (see below). If the strings have become twisted, smooth out. Overlap ends and secure well.

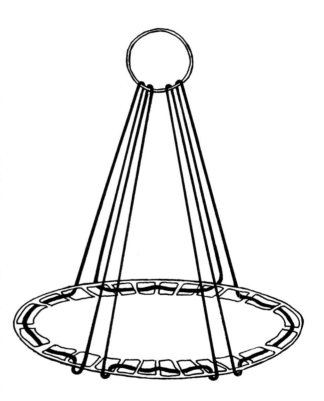

Weave braid through outer loops and four times through larger ring.

With raffia and larger hook, make 4 spirals, as follows: ch 34. Into 2nd ch from hook, work (1sc, 1hdc, 2dc), 4dc into each foll ch to last ch, (2dc, 1hdc, 1sc) into last ch.

Tie ends into a small bow around 4 pairs of strings, approx 2 inches (5cm) up from loops.

Tablecloth (page 60); Tray Cloth (page 59); Lace Doilies (page 58) shown in both blue and white.

CHAPTER FOUR

Tea Time

LACE DOILY

 Made in the finest cotton thread, this doily is the perfect complement to a china tea set.

◆

MATERIALS

175 yards (160m) of a size 20 crochet cotton
(yarn shown: Coats Crochet Cotton No. 20)
(extra yarn if crocheted loosely)
Size 8 steel (1.25mm) hook

◆

GAUGE

1st 8 rounds = 3½ inches (9cm) dia

◆

MEASUREMENTS

Approx 10½ inches (27cm) dia

◆

INSTRUCTIONS

Ch 7. Join with sl st into circle.

Round 1: Ch 3 (1st st). Into circle work 1dc, ch 4, (2dc, ch4) 4 times, sl st into top of 3ch. (5 loops.)

Round 2: Sl st to and into 1st loop, ch 3, (2dc, ch 4, 3dc) into same loop, ch 5, *(3dc, ch 4, 3dc) into next loop, ch 5.
Rep from * to end, sl st into top of 3ch.

Round 3: Sl st to and into 1st 4ch loop (= 3sl st), ch 3, (2dc, ch 4, 3dc) into same loop, ch 6, skip (3dc, ch 5, and foll 3dc), *(3dc, ch 4, 3dc) into next ch 6, skip (3dc, ch 5, and foll 3dc).
Rep from * to end, sl st into top of 3ch.

Round 4: 3sl st, ch 3, (2dc, ch 4, 3dc) into same loop, ch 10, *(3dc, ch 4, 3dc) into next 4ch loop, ch 10.
Rep from * to end, sl st into top of 3ch.

Round 5: 2sl st, 2sl st into loop, ch 3, 2dc into same loop, *ch 6, 1sc into 1st ch st of next 10ch, ch 12, 1sc under 3 loops below (enclosing 5ch, 6ch, and 10ch of prev 3 rounds), ch 12, 1sc into last ch st of same 10ch of prev round, ch 6, 3dc into next 4ch loop.
Rep from * omitting last 3dc at end of round, sl st into top of 3ch.

Round 6: 1sl st into center dc of 1st grp, ch 8, *skip next 6ch loop, 1sc into 1st of next 2 12ch loops, ch 7, 1sc into next 12ch loop, ch 7, skip next 6ch loop, 1sc into next center dc, ch 7.
Rep from * omitting last (sc and 7ch) at end of

round, sl st into 1st of 8ch.

Round 7: 1sl st into 1st 7ch loop, ch 2 (1st st), 5hdc into same loop, ch 4, *6hdc into next 7ch loop, ch 4. Rep from * to end, sl st into top of 2ch.

Round 8: Ch 3, 1dc into each of next 5hdc, (1hdc, ch 1, 1hdc) into next 4ch loop, *1dc into each of next 6hdc, (1hdc, ch 1, 1hdc) into next 4ch loop. Rep from * to end, sl st into top of 3ch.

Round 9: 8sl st to and into next 1ch sp, ch 7, 1dc into same sp, ch 7, *(1dc, ch4, 1dc) into next 1ch sp, ch 7. Rep from * to end, sl st into 3rd of 1st 7ch.

Round 10: 2sl st into 1st 4ch loop, ch 7, 1dc into same loop, ch 3, *(1dc, ch 4, 1dc) into 4th of next 7ch, ch 3, (1dc, ch 4, 1dc) into next 4ch loop, ch 3. Rep from * end, sl st into 3rd of 1st 7ch.

Round 11: 2sl st into 1st 4ch loop, ch 7, 1dc into same loop, (1dc, ch 4, 1dc) into next 3ch loop, *(1dc, ch 4, 1dc) into next 4ch loop, (1dc, ch 4, 1dc) into next 3ch loop.
Rep from * to end, sl st into 3rd of 7ch.

Round 12: 2sl st into 1st 4ch loop, ch 7, 1dc into same loop, *(1dc, ch 4, 1dc) into next 4ch loop.
Rep from * to end, sl st into 3rd of 7ch.

Rounds 13 and 14: Rep last round twice more.

Round 15: 1sl st into 1st 4ch sp, ch 3, 3dc into same sp, *4dc into next 4ch sp.
Rep from * to end, sl st into top of 3ch.

Round 16: *Ch 5, 1sc between next 2 4dc grps.
Rep from * to end. Do not sl st. (60 loops.)

Round 17: 2sl st into 1st 5ch loop, ch 3, (2dc, ch 4, 3dc) into same loop, ch 3, 1sc into next loop, ch 14, skip next loop, 1sc into next loop, ch 3, *(3dc, ch 4, 3dc) into next loop, ch 3, 1sc into next loop, ch 14, skip next loop, 1sc into next loop, ch 3.
Rep from * to end, sl st into top of 1st 3ch.

Round 18: 3sl st, ch 3, (2dc, ch 4, 3dc) into same 4ch loop, ch 13, skip 3 loops, *(3dc, ch 4, 3dc) into next 4ch loop, ch 13, skip 3 loops.
Rep from * to end, sl st into top of 3ch.

Round 19: 3sl st, ch 3, (2dc, ch 4, 3dc) into same 4ch loop, ch 16, skip 13ch, *(3dc, ch 4, 3dc) into next 4ch loop, ch 16, skip 13ch.
Rep from * to end, sl st into top of 3ch.

Round 20: 3sl st, ch 3, (2dc, ch 4, 3dc) into same

4ch loop, ch 17, skip 16ch, *(3dc, ch 4, 3dc) into next 4ch loop, ch 17, skip 16ch.

Rep from * to end, sl st into top of 3ch.

Round 21: 2sl st, 2sl st into loop, ch 3, 2dc into same loop, *ch 6, 1sc into 1st ch st of next 17ch, ch 13, 1sc under 4 loops below (enclosing 14ch, 13ch, 16ch, and 17ch of prev 4 rounds), ch 13, 1sc into last ch st of same 17ch, ch 6, 3dc into next 4ch loop. Rep from * omitting last 3dc at end of round, sl st into top of 3ch.

Round 22: 1sl st into center dc of 1st grp, ch 8, *skip next 6ch loop, 1hdc into 1st of next 2 13ch loops, ch 7, 1hdc into next 13ch loop, ch 7, skip next 6ch loop, 1sc into next center dc, ch 7.

Rep from * omitting last (sc and ch 7) at end of round, sl st into 1st of 8ch.

Round 23: Ch 3, 2dc into last sl st made, ch 3, 3dc into 1st 7ch loop, ch 3, *(3dc into next hdc, ch 3, 3dc into next 7ch loop, ch 3) twice, "3dc into next sc, ch 3, 3dc into next 7ch loop, ch 3."

Rep from * omitting " to " at end of round.

Round 24: 1sl st into center dc of 1st grp, ch 3, 2dc into last sl st made, ch 3, *3dc into next center dc, ch 3. Rep from * to end.

TRAY CLOTH
✳ ✳

Using sewing thread for the final round of the border gives this diamond-patterned tray cloth extra definition, especially if a strongly contrasting color is chosen.

◆

MATERIALS

370 yards (340m) of a size 10 crochet cotton
(yarn shown: DMC Cordonnet Spécial No. 10)
Sewing thread in contrasting color
Size 7 steel (1.50mm) hook

◆

GAUGE

8½ loops = 4 inches (10cm) across

◆

MEASUREMENTS

19 × 13½ inches (49 × 34cm)

◆

INSTRUCTIONS

Ch 153.

Row 1: 1sc into 9th ch from hook, *ch 5, skip next 3ch, 1sc into next ch. Rep from * to end, turn.

Row 2: Ch 5, 1sc into 1st 5ch sp, *ch 5, 1sc into next sp. Rep from * until all 37 loops have been worked into, ch 2, 1dc into 4th of last 8ch, turn.

Row 3: Ch 5, skip next 2ch, *1sc into next 5ch sp, ch 5. Rep from * to last loop, skip 1st 2ch of loop, 1sc into next ch, turn.

Row 4: Ch 5, 1sc into 1st 5ch sp, *ch 5, 1sc into next sp.

Rep from * until all loops have been worked into, ch 2, 1dc into end ch, turn.

Row 5: (RS) Ch 5, skip next 2ch, 1sc into next sp, (ch 5, 1sc) into each of next 2 sps, (5dc into next sc = fan), 1sc into next sp, *patt 5 (ch 5, 1sc) loops, fan, 1sc into next sp.

Rep from * to last 3 loops, patt 2 loops, ch 5, 1sc into 3rd of next 5ch, turn.

Row 6: As Row 4, but work 1sc into center dc of each fan, where they occur.

Row 7: Ch 5, skip next 2ch, 1sc into next sp, (patt 1 loop, fan, 1sc into next sp) twice, *patt 3 loops, fan, 1sc into next sp, patt 1 loop, fan, 1sc into next sp. Rep from * to last 2 loops, patt 1 loop, ch 5, 1sc into 3rd of next 5ch, turn.

Row 8: As Row 6.

Row 9: As Row 5.

Row 10: As Row 6.

Row 11: Patt 6 loops, *fan, 1sc into next sp, patt 5 loops. Rep from * to last loop, ch 5, 1sc into 3rd of next 5ch, turn.

Rows 12–15: Cont patt, completing the 5 diamonds as set over the next 2 RS rows. (End even rows with the ch 2, 1dc, as Row 4, and odd rows with ch 5, 1sc, as Row 5.)

Row 16: As Row 6.

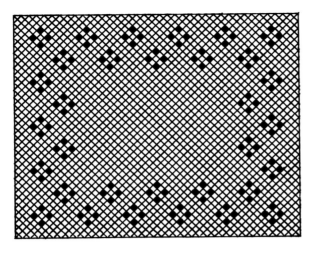

Chart for tray cloth

Row 17: Patt 3 loops, fan, 1sc into next sp. Work the (ch 5, 1sc) loop patt to last 4 loops, fan, 1sc into next sp, patt to end, turn.

Follow chart above, working fans on every RS row. Include 3 rows of loops after last fan row.

Final row: Ch 4, *1sc into next 5ch sp, ch 3. Rep from * to last loop, 1sc into 3rd of 5ch. Do not turn.

EDGING

Round 1: Start work along short side: ch 2, 2sc into 1st (half) loop sp, *1sc into next (full) loop sp, 2sc into next (half) loop sp. Rep from * to next corner.

Long side: ch 2, 2sc into 1st sp, *1sc into next sc stem, 3sc into next sp. Rep from * to 3rd corner. Ch 2 at corners and complete as above.

Round 2: Sl st into 1st 2ch sp, ch 3 (dc), 4dc into same sp. Work 1dc into each foll sc and 5dc into each foll 2ch sp, 1sc into top of 3ch.

Round 3: **(Over rem 4 corner dc, ch 3, skip next dc, 1sc into next dc) twice, *ch 4, skip next 2dc, 1sc into next dc.

Rep from * to next corner, then rep from ** to end. Sl st into base of 1st 3ch.

Round 4: 2sl st into 1st 3ch sp, ch 5, *1sc into next sp, ch 5.

Rep from * to end, sl st into 2nd of 2sl st.

Round 5: 1sl st into 1st sp, (ch 3, 1sc into same sp) twice, ch 3, 1sc into next sp (3 3ch loops made), *ch 5, 1sc into next sp.

Rep from * to end, but around each corner work 2 3ch loops into corner loop and 1 3ch loop each side of same loop (4 3ch loops). At end, complete 1st corner with 3ch loop, sl st into sl st.

Round 6: 1sl st into next sp, ch 5, *1sc into next sp, 5ch. Rep from * to end, sl st into sl st. Break yarn.

Round 7: With sewing threads, work 1sc into each st to end. Sl st.

Fasten off. Sew in ends.

TABLECLOTH
✳✳✳

This large and beautiful piece is made from repeated motifs, joined together as they are worked to avoid unsightly seams. An edging adds the finishing touch.

MATERIALS

2,500 yards (2,240m) of a size 20 crochet cotton
(yarn shown: Coats No. 20)
Size 8 steel (1.25mm) hook

GAUGE

Work to complete one motif to equal approx 3 inches (7cm) sq

MEASUREMENTS

Approx 36 inches (90cm) sq
(175 yards [160m] = approx 14 motifs)

INSTRUCTIONS FOR INDIVIDUAL MOTIFS

(See Fig. 1)

Ch 4. Join with sl st into circle.

Round 1: Ch 12, 1sl st into 5th ch from hook (loop), ch 3, (1tr into 1st circle, ch 8, 1sl st into 5th ch from hook, ch 3) 3 times, 1sc into 4th of 1st 12ch. (4 sps.)

Round 2: (Skip next 3ch, 9dc into next loop, skip next 3ch, 1sc into next tr) 4 times.

Round 3: Ch 5 (tr + 1ch), 1tr into same place as

One 5ch loop at center corner

One 3ch loop at center side

Fig. 1 Tablecloth motif

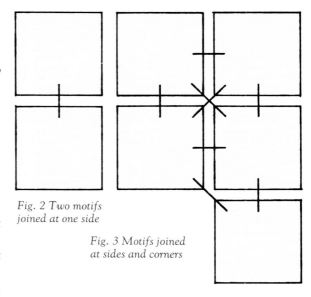

Fig. 2 Two motifs joined at one side

Fig. 3 Motifs joined at sides and corners

5ch, *ch 5, (1sc, ch 3, 1sc) into center dc of next 9dc, ch 5, (1tr, ch 1, 1tr) into next sc.

Rep from * to end, omitting last (1tr, ch 1, 1tr) at end of round, sl st into 4th of 1st 5ch.

Round 4: *(1sc, ch 3, 1sc) into next 1ch sp, ch 3, 9dc into next 3ch loop, ch 3.

Rep from * to end, sl st into 1st 3ch loop.

Round 5: Ch 3 (dc), 8dc into same loop as 3ch, *ch 6, 1sc into center dc of next 9dc, ch 6, 9dc into next 3ch loop.

Rep from * to end, omitting last 9dc at end of round.

Round 6: (1sc, ch 3, 1sc) into 1st dc of 1st 9dc, *ch 5, (1tr, ch 5, 1tr) into center dc of same 9dc, ch 5, (1sc, ch 3, 1sc) into 9th dc of same 9dc, ch 6, (1sc, ch 3, 1sc) into same place as next sc (center dc), ch 6, (1sc, ch 3, 1sc) into 1st dc of next 9dc.

Rep from * to end, omitting last (1sc, ch 3, 1sc) at end of round. Sl st into base of next 3ch.

JOINING MOTIFS

Work 1 motif. Complete 5 rounds of a 2nd motif. Join 2nd motif to 1st motif in one place—at center of 4th side of Rnd 6 (see Fig 2).

Motifs are joined on Rnd 6 by breaking into the 3ch loop at the center side or 5ch loop at center corner (see Fig 3, and Fig 4 overleaf), so instead of working (1sc, ch 3 for loop, 1sc) at center of 4th side on 2nd motif, work (1sc into 2nd motif, ch 1, 1sc into a corresponding 3ch loop on 1st motif (inserting hook from beneath), ch 1, 1sc into 2nd motif). Complete round to end. To join together motif corners, instead of working (1tr, ch 5, 1tr), work (1tr, ch 2, 1sc into a diagonally corresponding 5ch loop, ch 2, 1tr).

Where four corners meet, the first diagonal pair are joined as above; the second diagonal pair are joined as above, but enclose also the first pair with the 1sc (see Fig 3).

Continue to join motifs at sides and/or corners as and where necessary until cloth is 13 × 13 motifs square, or required size (see Fig. 4, page 62).

♦

EDGING

Round 1: With RS facing, and approx halfway between two tablecloth corners, join yarn to a 3ch loop at center-side of one motif.

Ch 11, 1sc into next 5ch corner sp, ch 3, *1sc into next 5ch corner sp on foll motif, ch 11, 1sc into next center-side loop, ch 11, 1sc into next 5ch corner sp, ch 3. Rep from * to next tablecloth corner. Form a corner loop by working another sc into same corner sp, ch 11, 1sc into next center-side loop.

Cont the patt until end of round. End with 1sc into 1st center-side loop.

Round 2: Ch 2, *(1sc, ch 2) 6 times into next 11ch sp, (1dc, ch 2) 6 times into next 3ch sp, (1sc, ch 2) 6 times into next 11ch sp.

Rep from * to end, 1sc into 1st loop.

Round 3: Ch 2, (1sc into next loop, ch 2) 5 times, *skip next 2ch. Between dcs, (1sc into next 2ch sp, ch 2) 5 times (= 4 loops), skip next 2ch, (1sc into next 2ch sp, ch 2) 11 times.

Rep from * to end, working (1sc, ch 2) only 6 times at end of round. 1sc into 1st loop.

Round 4: Cont with the (ch 2, 1sc) patt and, as before, ch 2 over 2ch at each side of dc gps (= 3 loops between 2 skipped 2ch).

End round with sl st.

Fig. 4 An attractive star pattern is created when corners are joined.

CAKE BAND

Dress up a special cake, English-style, with this pretty band, quickly and easily worked in cotton with ribbon trims.

◆

MATERIALS

283 yards (260m) of a size 10 crochet cotton
(yarn shown: DMC Cebelia No. 10)
Size 4 steel (1.75mm) hook
5 yards (4.7m) of ⅛ inch- (3mm-) wide satin
ribbon (6 × length of band plus extra for turning
under)
Matching sewing thread
Sewing needle
Tapestry needle

Scraps of narrow ribbon for bows (or pack of
10 small bows)

◆

GAUGE

34dc = 4 inches (10cm) across

◆

MEASUREMENTS

Approx 28½ × 3 inches (73 × 8cm)

◆

INSTRUCTIONS

Ch 215.

Row 1: 1dc into 4th ch from hook, 1dc into each foll ch to end, turn.

Row 2: Ch 3 (1st st), 1dc into each foll sp between dc to end, 1dc into end st, turn.

Row 3: Ch 3 (1st st), skip 1st sp, 1dc into each foll sp to last sp, skip sp, work 1dc into end st, turn.

Rows 4–6: Rep last 2 rows once more, then Row 2 again.

Row 7: (Ruffle) *Ch 15, 1sc into next st. Rep from * to ⅜ inch (1cm) from end. Break yarn and fasten off. With same side (RS) facing, join yarn ⅜ inch (1cm)

from end of base ch and rep last row to match opp side.

Thread ribbon onto tapestry needle and weave between dcs. Leave ¾ inch (2cm) extra at each end of ribbons. Cut and secure ends on WS.

Space 10 bows evenly along cake band and sew centers.

TEA COZY

Worked mainly in single and double crochet, this tea cozy has the advantage of a lining to help keep a teapot really hot. All around are twelve little cups hanging on hooks, with their saucers standing on a rack beneath. Some simple embroidery decorates the top, and a solid handle completes the picture. You could crochet the cozy in colors to complement a favorite tea set.

◆

MATERIALS

Knitting worsted (yarn shown: Patons Diploma Gold DK), 255 yards (230m) each of main color (MC) and contrasting color (CC)
127 yards (116m) of 3rd color for cups and saucers scraps of 4th color for rims
Size G/6 (4.50mm) hook for cozy, size E/4 (3.50mm) for dishes
Piece of broom handle or spool for cozy handle
Tapestry needle

◆

GAUGE

15sts and 14 rounds (over long and short st patt) = 14 inches (10cm)

◆

MEASUREMENTS

Height excluding handle = 7½ inches (19cm)
Inner and outer circumferences = 20 inches (52cm) and 21 inches (54cm)

◆

INSTRUCTIONS

With CC yarn and larger hook, ch 87. Join into untwisted circle with sl st.

Round 1: Ch 1 (1st sc), 1sc into each foll ch to end,

sl st into 1st sc. (87sts.)

Rounds 2–4: Ch 1 (1st sc), 1sc into each foll st to end, sl st into 1st sc.

Round 5: Join MC with 2ch (1st sc), 1sc into back top loop only of each foll st to end (hemline), sl st into top of 2ch.
Cont with MC.

Round 6: Ch 1 (1st sc), *1dc into next st, 1sc into foll st.
Rep from * to end, 1dc into 1st sc.

Rounds 7–23: Cont by working 1sc into each dc, and 1dc into each sc (long and short st), without sl st at end of each round, for 17 more rounds. End with 1sc. Change to CC. Work 1sl st into next st.

Round 24: Ch 1 (1st sc), sc to end, dec 3sts evenly over round, sl st into 1st sc.

Round 25: Ch 1 (1st sc), 1sc into each foll st to end, sl st into 1st sc.

Round 26: Ch 1 (1st sc), 1sc into next st, ch 5 (cup loop), *1sc into each of next 7sts, ch 5.
Rep from * to last 5sts, 5sc to end, sl st into 1st sc. (12 loops.)

Round 27: Ch 1 (1st sc). Bringing loops forward to RS, work 1sc into next sc and each foll sc to end. Change to MC, sl st into 1st sc. (84sts.)

Round 28: Ch 1 (1st sc), 1dc into next st, *1sc into next st, 1dc into foll st.
Rep from * to end, sl st into 1st sc.

Round 29: Ch 3 (1st dc), 1sc into next st, *1dc into next st, 1sc into foll st.
Rep from * to end.
Change to CC, sl st into top of 3ch.

Round 30: Ch 1 (1st sc), sc to end, dec 7sts evenly over round, sl st into 1st sc. (continued on page 66)

Cake Band (page 62); Napkin Rings (page 67);
Tea Cozy (page 63).

Rounds 31–33: Rep last round 3 times more, varying positions of decs. Change to MC for sl st of final round.

Rounds 34–35: Rep Rnds 28 and 29 once more.

Round 36: (CC) Ch 1 (1st sc), sc to end, dec 11 sts evenly over round, sl st into 1st sc.

Round 37: As last round. Change to MC for sl st of round.

Rounds 38–40: Rep Rnds 28 and 29 once, then Rnd 28 again. (34sts.)

Break off MC and cont in CC, without sl st to end (see below).

♦

LINING

Rounds 41–43: Sc to end. Cont in hdc throughout.

Rounds 44–47: Inc 10sts evenly over each round (74sts.)

Round 48: Hdc to end.

Round 49: Inc 8sts over round.

Round 50 and 51: Hdc to end.

Round 52: Inc 3sts over round.

Cont on these sts until lining, when folded through to inside, reaches approx ⅜ inch (1cm) from hemline. End with 2sc, 1 sl st.

Break yarn and fasten off. Darn in all ends except last end, to allow for any adjustment that may be needed.

Smooth out both fabrics. Insert pins from RS to hold lining evenly in place. Fold first few rounds (CC) of cozy base to inside, allowing hemline to sit neatly at edge.

Enclose base of lining inside, adjusting lining length if necessary, and stitch hem.

♦

SAUCER RACK

(Using larger hook, CC yarn.)

Ch 90. Join with sl st into circle. (Check for fit around widest part of cozy and if necessary adjust no. of ch, which must be divisible by 3.)

Round 1: Ch 1 (1st sc), 1sc into each foll ch to end, sl st into 1st sc.

Round 2: Ch 4 (1st hdc + 2ch), skip next 2sts, *1hdc into next st, ch 2, skip next 2sts.

Rep from * to end, sl st into 2nd of 4ch.

Round 3: 4sc into each 2ch sp to end, sl st into 1st sc. Fasten off.

♦

SAUCER

(Using smaller hook, 3rd col yarn, make 12.)

Wind yarn once around little finger, slip off,

Begin saucer with a loop to avoid a center hole

holding circle. Insert hook through center and draw yarn through to front (see above).

Round 1: Ch 1, 6sc into circle. Pull free end to close circle, sl st into 1st sc. (6sts.)

Round 2: Ch 1 (1st sc), 1sc into same place as 1ch, 2sc into each foll sc to end, sl st into 1st sc. (12sts.)

Round 3: Ch 1 (1st sc), 1sc into next st, 2sc into foll st, (1sc into each of next 2sts, 2sc into foll st) 3 times, sl st into 1st sc.

Round 4: Ch 1 (1st sc), 1sc into each of next 2sts, 2sc into next st, (1sc into each of next 3sts, 2sc into foll st) 3 times, sl st into 1st sc.

Round 5: Ch 1 (1st sc), 2sc into next st, (1sc into each of next 4sts, 2sc into next st) 3 times, work 3sc to end, sl st into 1st sc. Break off yarn.

Round 6: With 4th col yarn, work 1 round of sl st on WS, for rim. Fasten off.

Back-stitch a circle with tapestry needle between 1st two rounds.

♦

CUP

(Using smaller hook, 3rd col yarn, make 12.)

Ch 3. Join with sl st into circle.

Round 1: Ch 1, 6sc into circle, sl st into 1st sc. (6sts.)

Round 2: Ch 1 (1st sc). Working into back top loop of sc for this round only, 1sc into next st, 2sc into next st, 1sc into each of next 2sts, 2sc into next st, sl st into 1st sc.

Round 3: Ch 1 (1st sc), (2sc into next st, 1sc into foll st) 3 times, 2sc into last st, sl st into 1st sc.

Round 4: Ch 1 (1st sc), 1sc into each of next 2sts, (2sc into next st, 1sc into each of next 3sts) twice, 2sc into last st, sl st into 1st sc.

Round 5: Ch 1 (1st sc), 1sc into each of next 4sts, 2sc into next st, 1sc into each of next 6sts, 2sc into next st, sc to end, sl st into 1st sc. (17sts.)

Rounds 6 and 7: Ch 1 (1st sc), sc to end, sl st into 1st sc.

Ch 9 for handle, 1sl st into single loop at back of 2nd ch from hook, and each of next 7ch.

Break off 3rd col yarn.

Round 8: (Rim) With 4th col yarn, ch 1, 1sc into each st of Rnd 7, sl st into 1st sc. Break yarn and fasten off.

◆

HANDLE

(Using larger hook, CC yarn, make a cover for spool.)

Ch 3. Join with sl st into circle.

Round 1: Ch 3 (1st dc), 11dc into circle, sl st into top of 3ch.

Round 2: Ch 1 (1st sc), 2sc into next st, *1sc into next st, 2sc into foll st.

Rep from * to end, sl st into 1st sc. Without inc, work sc rounds to length of spool using a different color (of the 4 colors used) for each round.

Break off yarns and sew in ends.

Make a second circle for top of spool and sew all tog around spool. Gather cozy top around handle and sew securely. With MC and tapestry needle,

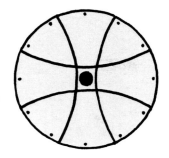

Bird's-eye view of the cozy, with handle at center, showing position for four arcs of stitching.

work 4 arcs of stem stitch across top of cozy, using doubled yarn (see above).

Pin saucers evenly around cozy 1 inch (2.5cm) from cozy base. Sew on close to centers.

Work a round of back stitch attaching rack base to cozy, so that saucer bases show through holes. Work another round, near top of rack, catching rims of saucers twice. Thread cup handles through loops and sew in place.

NAPKIN RINGS

✳✳

Once you have mastered the knack of making these simple "popcorn" motifs, you will find it quick and easy to make them into pretty napkin rings.

◆

MATERIALS

870 yards (800m) of a firmly twisted size 3 crochet cotton (yarn shown: Twilleys Secco No. 3) (enough for 6 napkin rings)
Size E/4 (3.50mm) hook
⅝ yard (50cm) of ¼ inch- (8mm-) wide double-faced satin ribbon
Tapestry needle

◆

POPCORN MOTIF

Ch 6. Join with sl st into circle, ch 3 (dc), 4dc into circle.

To make a popcorn, remove hook from last (5th) dc, insert hook from front into top of 1st of the 5dc (behind 2nd, 3rd, and 4th dc), catch loop of 5th dc on hook, and draw through. Keep fairly tight.

Ch 3, (5dc into circle, make a popcorn with these

5dc, ch 3) 5 times. Sl st into closing st behind 1st popcorn. Break yarn and fasten off.

Make another popcorn motif, but instead of working the final ch 3, ch 1, sl st into any 3ch loop of prev motif, ch 1 again, then sl st into closing st behind 1st popcorn.

Join on 2 more motifs so that there are 4 motifs in a straight line.

To form a ring, join a 5th motif to last and 1st motifs by interrupting both 3rd and final 3ch loop with the ch 1, 1sl st, ch 1 as before.

Using tapestry needle, thread a line of ribbon over joined ch loops and behind each motif (see below). Pull ribbon up very slightly through center holes, and make a small stitch underneath ribbon and across hole to secure. Tie ends in a small bow.

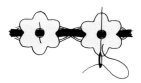

Thread ribbon over loops and behind each motif

CHAPTER FIVE

The Bedroom

Bedspread (page 70); Hot Water Bottle Cover (page 71);
Filet Bed Linen Edgings (page 72).

BEDSPREAD

✽ ✽ ✽

For this elegant bedspread, motifs made of ovals within long hexagons are crocheted together to create a pretty fabric, which is then adorned with decorative fringe around the edge.

◆

MATERIALS

Sport-weight cotton yarn:
10,450 yards (9,600m) for standard twin bed
13,350 yards (12,250m) for standard double bed
Size E/4 (3.50m) hook

◆

GAUGE

1st 3 rounds = 3 × 2½ inches (7.7 × 6.3cm)

◆

MOTIF

Approx 7 × 6 inches (18 × 16cm)
45 yards (40m) = 1 motif
Twin bedspread 175 motifs
Double bedspread 229 motifs

◆

MEASUREMENTS

(excluding fringe)
104 × 70 inches (264 × 180cm) twin size
104 × 90 inches (264 × 232cm) double size

◆

OVAL/HEXAGON MOTIF

Ch 6. Join with sl st into circle.

Round 1: Ch 3 (1st dc). Into circle, work 5dc, 3tr, 6dc, 3tr. Sl st into top of 3ch.

Round 2: 1sl st between 1st 2dc, ch 2 (1st hdc), 1hdc into 2nd ch from hook, (1hdc between next 2 sts. Work 1hdc into last sp made by inserting hook, from front, around stem of last hdc made = half double pair, called hp). Cont in this way by working 1hp into each foll sp between sts to end, sl st into top of 2ch. (18hdc pairs.)

Round 3: (1sl st into next st, 1sl st into 1st sp = 2sl st), ch 2 (1st hdc), 1hdc into 2nd ch from hook, 1hp into each of next 5sps (of rem 17sps between hps), 2 hp (inc) into next sp, 1hp into each of next 8sps, 2hp into next sp, 1hp into each of next 2sps, sl st into top of 2ch. (20hp.)

Round 4: 2sl st, ch 2 (1st hdc), 1hdc into 2nd ch from hook, 1hp into each of next 4sps, 2hp into next sp, 1hp into each of next 9sps, 2hp into next

sp, 1hp into each of next 4sps, sl st into top of 2ch. (22hp.) Pull to shape.

Round 5: 2sl st, ch 2 (1st hdc), (1sc, 1hdc) into 2nd ch from hook, (1hdc into next sp. Work both 1sc and 1hdc into last sp made, inserting hook, from front, around stem of last hdc made = single crochet half double pair, or shp). 1shp into each of next 4sps, 2shp into each of next 2sps, 1shp into each of next 9sps, 2shp into each of next 2sps, 1shp into each of next 3sps, sl st into 1st sc. (26shp.) Cont to pull gently into shape.

Round 6: 2sl st, ch2 (1st hdc), (1sc, 2hdc) into 2nd ch from hook (1hdc into next sp—under 3 strands. Work 1sc and 2hdc into last sp made, around stem of last hdc made = single crochet half double half double pair, or shhp), 1shhp into each foll sp to end, sl st into top of 2ch. (26 shhp.)

Round 7: (Ch 4, 1sc tightly into next sp) to end. (26 loops.)

Round 8: 1sl st into 1st 4ch sp, ch 3 (1st dc), 1hdc into 2nd ch from hook, ch 3.
Into same 4ch sp, work (1dc, 1hdc around stem of last dc = called double half double pair, or dh), ch 1, **(1dh, ch 1) into next sp, (1hp, ch 1) into each of next 2sps, (1dh, ch 1) into next sp, (1dh, ch 3, 1dh, ch 1) into next sp, (1hp, ch 1) into each of next 2sps, (1dh, ch 3, 1dh, ch 1) into next sp, (1dh, ch 1) into next sp, (1hp, ch 1) into each of next 2sps, (1dh, ch 1) into next sp, *(1dh, ch 3, 1dh, ch 1) into next sp.
Rep from ** to * once more, sl st into top of 1st 3ch.

Round 9: 2sl st, ch 3 (1st dc), 1hdc into 2nd ch from hook, ch 3, 1dh into same sp, ch 1.
Cont to end with (1dh, ch 1) into each 1ch sp, and (1dh, ch 3, 1dh, ch 1) into each 3ch sp. Sl st into top of 1st 3ch.

◆

LAYOUT AND JOINING MOTIFS

The 2 shorter sides of motifs are laid parallel with head and foot ends of bed. Beg and ending with a 13-motif line, the bedpsread is made with alternate lines of 13 and 14 motifs running from head to foot, the 14-motif lines being ½ motif longer each end. For a twin-size bedspread, make 13 of these lines. For a double size, make 17 lines.
Motifs are crocheted together on RS by working

(1sc, ch 2) into each 1ch sp, and (2sc, ch 1—center, 2sc, ch 2) into each 3ch sp as follows:

Place WS of 2 motifs together. Join yarn into 3ch sp at start of one shorter side and ch 2 for the 1st sc. Work 1sc into same sp, ch 2 (1sc, ch2) into each of next 4 1ch sps, (2sc, ch 1) into next 3ch sp.

A 3rd motif is now attached at a 3ch sp between two longer sides—disregard the 2nd (farthest) motif, and join on the 3rd motif by working 2sc into both the same sp of 1st motif and the relevant 3ch sp of 3rd motif. Ch 2, (1sc, ch2) into each of next 6sps of 1st and 3rd motifs, (2sc, ch 1) into next sp. Join on a 4th motif.

Cont attaching motifs in this way. When a 3ch sp is already partially joined to another motif, work only 2sc and, into the 1ch center sp already made, 1sc to attach. Each 3ch sp, therefore, will have (2sc, ch 1, 2sc) or (2sc, 1sc into a 1ch center sp, 2sc).

◆

FRINGE

Cut 10-inch (25cm) lengths of yarn.

Fold 4 lengths together at center, insert fold from front into a 1ch sp at edge of bedspread and thread ends through. Pull ends to make a fairly tight and even knot.

Use 6 strands for the 3ch sps that fall on the lower or outer part of motifs. Work these tassels into every sp at edge of 2 long and 1 short side of spread. Join tassels together by taking 2 strands of yarn from one side of a tassel, and 2 nearest strands from the adjacent tassel. Tie tightly together with a square knot, leaving a small fingertip space between knot and motif. Complete to end. Trim fringe even, following the outer line of motifs.

HOT WATER BOTTLE COVER

 Just the thing for a winter's night. The small gaps left by this pattern allow plenty of heat to filter through to where it is needed.

◆

MATERIALS

447 yards (410m) of a sport-weight yarn (yarn shown: Patons Knit 'n' Save)
Size F/5 (4.00mm) hook

◆

GAUGE

Doubled fabric should measure approx 10 inches (25cm) across

◆

MEASUREMENTS

Approx 14 × 10 inches (36 × 25cm)

◆

INSTRUCTIONS

Ch 108. Join with sl st into circle.

Round 1: Ch 3 (hdc + 1ch), 1hdc into same place as 3ch, skip next 2ch, *(1hdc, ch 1, 1hdc) into next ch, skip next 2ch.

Rep from * to end, sl st into 2nd of 3ch.

Round 2: Sl st into 1st 1ch sp, ch 3, 1hdc into same sp, *(1hdc, ch 1, 1hdc) into next 1ch sp.

Rep the "V" patt from * to end, sl st into 2nd of 3ch.

Round 3: Sl st into 1st 1ch sp, ch 3, 1hdc into same sp. Inc a "V" by working (1hdc, ch1, 1hdc) into sp between last and next "V," (1hdc, ch 1, 1hdc) into each of next 18 1ch sps, inc a "V" into sp between last and next "V," (1hdc, ch 1, 1hdc) into each foll 1ch sp to end, sl st into 2nd of 3ch.

Rep Rnd 2 until work measures 14 inches (35cm) from base ch.

Final round: Sl st into 1st 1ch sp, ch 2 (1st hdc), 4hdc into same sp. Remove hook from last hdc of this 5hdc grp, insert hook (from front) into 1st hdc of grp, catch unhooked loop of 5th hdc and draw through to close top (popcorn made). Ch 1.

Work a 5hdc popcorn and ch 1 into each foll 1ch sp to end, sl st into top of 2ch. Break yarn and fasten off. Turn work WS out and darn in ends. With the Rnd 3 incs placed at each side, sew base, gathering fabric slightly during first and last few sts. Turn RS out. Make a twisted cord for neck (see Techniques) and thread through sps at each side of "V"s, approx 11 rounds from top.

FILET BED LINEN EDGINGS

✳✳

🍀 *Transform even the plainest sheets and pillowcases—for yourself or your guests—with these attractive filet crochet edgings.*

◆

FILET

Sp = 1dc, ch 2, 1dc. Change the 2ch to 2dc to form a block of 4dc. (Last st of sq counts as 1st st of next sq.) For further instructions on filet crochet, see p. 11.

◆

MATERIALS

Sheet

800 yards (740m) of a size 20 crochet cotton
(yarn shown: DMC Cebelia No. 20)
Size 7 steel (1.50mm) hook

Pillowcase

160 yards (150m) of a size 2 crochet cotton
Size 7 steel (1.50mm) hook
Approx 20 inches (50cm) narrow double-faced
satin ribbon

Matching sewing thread
Sewing needle

◆

GAUGE/MEASUREMENTS

Sheet

(Without ch and picot edging)
Width = 4 and 5½ inches (10 and 13.5cm) at
narrowest and widest points
12-row patt = 2½ inches (6.5cm)

Pillowcase

(With ch edging)
Width = 2 inches (5.5cm)
at widest point
6-row patt = 1¼ inches (3cm)

◆

INSTRUCTIONS FOR SHEET

Ch 51.

Row 1: 1dc into 4th ch from hook, 1dc into each

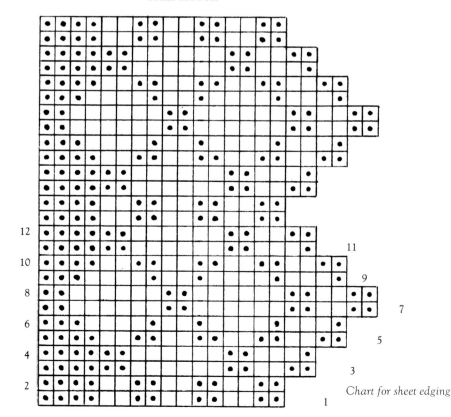

Chart for sheet edging

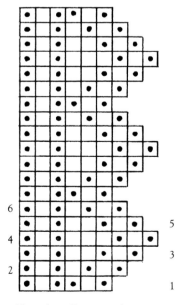

Chart for pillowcase edging

72

of next 5ch, *(ch 2, skip next 2ch, 1dc into next ch) twice, 1dc into each of next 6ch.

Rep from * twice more. Work 1dc into each of next 6ch, turn.

Follow chart (see below left) from Row 2, shaping as shown. Patt repeats after Row 12.

Edging: Around pointed edge, work a picot of (1sc, ch 3, 1sc) into each inner and outer corner. Link the picots with 5ch and 6ch, respectively, along horizontal (dc sides) and vertical "steps" (dc tops). Across tips only, work 6ch between picots (see below).

Hand- or machine-stitch straight side of edging to edge of sheet.

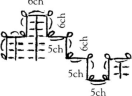

Sheet edging, showing picots at inner and outer corners, with linking chains

INSTRUCTIONS FOR PILLOWCASE

Ch 21.

Row 1: 1dc into 4th ch from hook, 1dc into each of next 2ch, ch 2, skip next 2ch, 1dc into each of next 7ch, ch 2, skip next 2ch, 1dc into each of next 4ch, turn.

Follow chart (see page 72, right) from Row 2, shaping as shown. Patt repeats after Row 6.

Edging: Join yarn to outer corner at start of 1st row, and work around points as follows:

(ch 3, 1sc) into each of next 3 outer corners, ch 3 across tip, 1sc into next corner (same block), (ch 3, 1sc) into each of next 2 corners, ch 3 across center, 1sc into next outer corner. Continue similarly to end.

Slot ribbon through sps at one block in from straight edge. Hem ends on WS of edging.

Hand-sew straight side of edging to open edge of pillowcase, through one thickness of pocketed fabric. Allow point tips to rest fairly close to fold.

DRESSING-TABLE SET

This deceptively simple network of chains is quickly worked into useful and attractive mats that lend the classic finishing touch to a dressing table.

MATERIALS

220 yards (200m) of a size 10 crochet cotton (yarn shown: Coats Crochet Cotton No. 10)
Size 4 steel (1.75mm) hook

MEASUREMENTS

Small mat 6½ × 6 inches (17 × 15cm)
Large mat 11 × 9½ inches (28 × 24cm)

INSTRUCTIONS

For small mat (make two), ch 66; for large mat, ch 116 (see page 74).

Row 1: 1sc into 11th ch from hook, ch 11, 1sc into same base ch as last sc, ch 5, skip next 4 base ch, 1sc into next ch, *ch 5, skip next 4 base ch, (1sc, ch 11, 1sc) into next ch, ch 5, skip next 4 base ch, 1sc into next ch. Rep from * to end, turn.

Row 2: Ch 7, skip 1st 5ch loop, 1sc into center (6th) ch st of next 11ch loop, ch 6, *1sc into sc between next 2 5ch loops, ch 6, skip next 5ch, 1sc into center ch st of next 11ch loop, ch 6.

Rep from * to end, skip remainder of 11ch loop and next 5ch, 1sc into next ch st, turn.

Row 3: Ch 10, 1sc into sc at tip of 1st 11ch loop, *ch 9, 1sc into sc at tip of next 11ch loop.

Rep from * ending row with 4ch, 1dtr into end ch st of next 7ch, turn.

Row 4: Ch 6, (1sc, ch 11, 1sc) into next sc, ch 5, *1sc into center ch st of next 9ch, ch 5, (1sc, ch 11, 1sc) into next sc, ch 5.

Rep from * to end, skip next 4ch, 1sc into next ch st, turn.

Small mat: Rep Rows 2–4, 5 times more.
Large mat: Rep Rows 2–4, 10 times more.
Both mats: Rep Rows 2 and 3, once more.

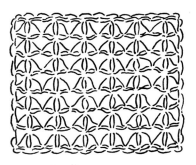

Small mat

Large mat

*Interlaced chains
produce a reversible fabric*

Final row: Ch 5, 1sc into next sc, ch 5, *1sc into center ch st of next 9ch, ch 5, 1sc into next sc, ch 5. Rep from * to end, skip next 4ch, 1sc into next ch st, turn.

♦

BORDER

1st side: Ch 5, 1sc into 1st 5ch sp, *ch 5, 1sc into next 5ch sp. Rep from * to end, ch 5, 1sc into top of dtr. Do not turn.

2nd side: Ch 5, 1sc into center of 1st triangle sp (around dtr stem), *ch 8, 1sc into identical triangle sp of next 3-row patt.

Rep from * to end, ch 5, 1sc into corner st. Complete rem sides to match.

TABLETOP OR CHEST COVER

✱ ✱

More-or-less filet crochet, the openwork row pattern of this cover creates very gentle scallops along each side.

♦

MATERIALS

450 yards (410m) of a size 5 crochet cotton (yarn shown: Twilleys Southern Comfort)
Size C/2 (2.50mm) hook
Sewing thread and needle
Piece of carboard, 4 inches (11cm) sq

♦

GAUGE

29dc and 13 rows = 4 inches (10cm) sq

♦

MEASUREMENTS

19½ × 14 inches (50 × 36cm)

♦

INSTRUCTIONS

Ch 98 (or any no. divisible by 10 minus 2), not too tightly.

Row 1: 1dc into 4th ch from hook, 1dc into each foll ch to end, turn.

Row 2: Ch 3 (1st st), 1dc into next st, ch 2, skip next 2sts, *1dc into each of next 8sts, ch 2, skip next 2sts. Rep from * to last 2sts, 2dc, turn.

Row 3: Ch 3 (1st st), 1dc into next st, ch 2, skip next 2ch, *1dc into each of next 8sts, ch 2, skip next 2ch. Rep from * to last 2sts, 2dc, turn.

Rows 4–9: Rep last row, 6 times more.

Row 10: Ch 3 (1st st), 1dc into next st, ch 2, skip next 2ch, *1dc into each of next 3sts, ch 2, skip next 2sts, 1dc into each of next 3 sts, ch 2, skip next 2ch. Rep from * to last 2 sts, 2dc, turn.

Row 11: Ch 3 (1st st), 1dc into next st, ch 2, skip next 2ch, *1dc into next st, ch 2, skip next 2sts, 2dc into next sp, ch 2, skip next 2sts, 1dc into next st, ch 2, skip next 2ch.
Rep from * to last 2sts, 2dc, turn.

Row 12: Ch 3 (1st st), 1dc into next st, ch 2, skip next 2ch, *1dc into next st, 2dc into next sp, ch 2, skip next 2sts, 2dc into next sp, 1dc into next st, ch 2, skip next 2ch.
Rep from * to last 2sts, 2dc, turn.

Row 13: Ch 3 (1st st), 1dc into next st, ch 2, skip next 2ch, *1dc into each of next 3sts, 2dc into next sp, 1dc into each of next 3sts, ch 2, skip next 2ch. Rep from * to last 2sts, 2dc, turn. Rep Rows 3–13, 5 times more (or to desired length, less approx 2 inches [5cm]). Rep Row 3, 7 times more.

Final row: Ch 3 (1st st), 1dc into next st, 2dc into next sp, *1dc into each of next 8sts, 2dc into next sp. Rep from * to last 2 sts, 2dc.

Break yarn and fasten off.

Working along base row toward slipknot at 1st corner, rejoin yarn at sp between 10th and 11th dc from same corner, ch 1, 1sc into sp between 9th and 10th dc, ch 3, 1sc into next sp, (ch 4, 1sc) into each of next 2sps, (ch 5, 1sc) into each of next 3sps, (ch 6, 1sc) into each of next 2sps, ch 8, 1sc again into final sp. Do not turn.

Cont around corner along side: ch 7, 1sc into sp between 2dc at end of 2nd row, ch 6, 1sc into same sp, (ch 5, 1sc) into each of next 2sps, ch 4, 1sc into next sp, ch 3, 1sc into same sp, ch 3, 1sc into next sp, ch 2, 1sc into same sp, ch 2, 1sc into each of next 2sps. (Ending at 8th row.)

Complete diagonally opp corner to match. Match rem corners, starting at 8th rows (see below).

TASSEL TOP

(Make 4.)

Ch 4. Join with sl st into circle.

Round 1: Work 8sc into circle.

Rounds 2–5: Sc to end. (8sts.)

Round 6: 1sl st into next st, *ch 1, 1sl st into next st. Rep from * to end. Break yarn and fasten off, leaving an 8-inch (20cm) end for stitching.

To complete a tassel, wind some yarn 30 times around the piece of carboard. Remove, and fit loop ends into tassel top opening. Gather around edge, and sew to secure. Cut open rem loops. Sew tassels to 8ch loops at corners of cover.

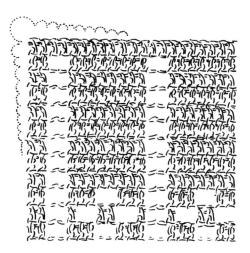

Pattern sketch of the cover, showing loops increasing in size toward one corner

SMALL CUSHION
✻✻

A small variation of single crochet produces the firm fabric that makes up most of this neat little cushion. Two lengths of pointed edging, one in each color, are made separately, joined along the pointed side and lightly padded. Decorated cords complete the cushion.

MATERIALS

Knitting worsted-weight cotton yarn (yarn shown: Jaeger Cotton DK), 490 yards (450m) of main color (MC) and 245 yards (225m) of contrasting color (CC)
Sizes F/5, E/4, and D/3 (4.00, 3.50, and 3.00mm) hooks
Invisible sewing thread
Tapestry and sewing needles
Small amount of batting for pendant and border
Pillow form

GAUGE

19sts and 21 rows - 4 inches (10cm) sq

MEASUREMENTS

Excluding border, 13 × 14 inches (33 × 36cm)

METHOD

(Two pieces alike)
With MC and largest hook, ch 51.
Row 1: (RS) 1sc into 2nd ch from hook, 1sc into each foll ch to end, turn (50sts.)
Row 2: Ch 2 (1st st), 1sc into 1st st to make an increased st, 1sc into each of next 2sts, *1sc into back top loop of next st, 1sc into front top loop of foll st.

ABOVE: Dressing-table Set (page 73)

RIGHT: Small Cushion (this page); Tabletop or Chest Cover (page 74)

Rep from * to last 3sts, (both loops) 1sc into next st, 2sc into next st, 1sc into final st, turn.

Cont to work the few sts at each end in normal sc.

Row 3: Ch 2 (1st st), 1sc into 1st st (inc), 1sc into each of next 2sts, *1sc into front top loop of next st, 1sc into back top loop of foll st.

Rep from * to last 3sts, 1sc into next st, 2sc into next st, 1sc into final st, turn.

Rows 4–7: Rep last 2 rows twice more. (62sts.)

Row 8: Ch 1 (1st st), 1sc into each of next 2sts, *1sc into back top loop of next st, 1sc into front top loop of foll st. Rep from * to last 3sts, 3sc, turn.

Rep last row until work measures approx 10¼ inches (26cm). End with WS row.

Decrease edges as follows:

Row 1: (RS) Ch 2 (1st st), sc2tog, 1sc into next sc, *1sc into front top loop of next st, 1sc into back top loop of foll st.

Rep from * to last 4sts, 1sc into next st, sc2tog, 1sc into final sc, turn.

Row 2: Ch 2 (1st st), sc2tog, 1sc into next st, *1sc into back top loop of next st, 1sc into front top loop of foll st.

Rep from * to last 4sts, 1sc into next st, sc2tog, 1sc into final st, turn.

Rep last 2 rows until 50 sts remain.

◆

INNER BORDER

Round 1: Working in normal sc, join CC yarn and ch 2 (1st st), 1sc into 1st st (inc), *work 48sc to last st, 2sc into next st.

Do not turn. Work along decreased edge.

5sc to next point, 2sc into next st, 36sc evenly along (straight) side, 2sc into next point, 5sc along increased edge, 2sc into start of base ch.

Cont to end of round, matching first 2 sides. Omit the final 2sc. End with sl st into top of 1st 2ch.

Round 2: Ch 1 (1st st), sc to end, change color, sl st into 1st st.

Round 3: (MC) As Rnd 2 but inc 1 st at each of the 8 "corners," change color, sl st into 1st st.

Round 4: (CC) As Rnd 2 (without color change).

Round 5: (CC) As Rnd 3.

Break yarn and fasten off.

◆

POINTED BORDER

(Make one of each color.)

With same hook, ch 3.

Row 1: 1sc into 2nd ch from hook, 1sc into next ch, turn.

Row 2: Ch 1 (1st st), 1sc into next st, turn.

Row 3: Ch 3, 1sc into 2nd ch from hook, 1sc into next ch, 2sc to end, turn.

Row 4: Ch 1 (1st st), 3sc to end, turn.

Row 5: Ch 3, 1sc into 2nd ch from hook, 1sc into next ch, 4sc to end, turn.

Row 6: Ch 1 (1st st), 5sc to end, turn.

Row 7: Ch 3, 1sc into 2nd ch from hook, 1sc into next ch, 6sc to end, turn.

Rows 8 and 9: Ch 1 (1st st), 1sc into each of next 5sts, turn.

Rows 10 and 11: Ch 1 (1st st), 1sc into each of next 3sts, turn.

Rows 12 and 13: Ch 1 (1st st), 1sc into next st, turn.

Rep Rows 2–13 until 17 complete points have been worked. Break yarn and fasten off.

Place the 2 pointed borders together, with one slip-knot on lhs and other on rhs.

Leave each straight edge unworked. With either color yarn and same hook, join the stepped edges by picking up (both together) single loops from one color (inc rows) and two loops from second color (dec rows). Join at rhs, work 2sc up each of first 3 step sides, 1sl st into 1st st of 4th step side, 3sc into 2nd st of same step.

*Omit the tip, and work down 2nd side: 3sc into 1st st of same top step, 1sl st into 2nd st of same step, 2sc down each of 2nd and 3rd step sides, sc2tog (working into between-st at center and 1st of next 1st step), 1sc into 2nd st of 1st step, 2sc up next step, 1sl st into 1st st of next step, 3sc into 2nd st of same step (see below).

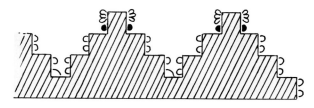

Stitch placement for the pointed border

Rep from * to start of 2nd side of 17th point, 3sc into 1st st, 1sl st into 2nd st of top step, 2sc down each of next 3 steps. Break yarn and fasten off.

Using invisible thread, wind tightly around 2sl st "neck" at top of each point, making approx ⅓ inch (8mm) width (see page 79, top).

Sew ends to inside.

Completed shape after winding invisible thread around tip

Pad each point with triangle of ¼- to ½-inch- (5mm- to 1cm-) thick batting. Overcast loosely with either color of yarn all along base edge, to close. Baste straight edge of border with points outward to WS of one cushion piece, ½ inch (1cm) from cushion edge, around one long and two shorter sides, starting with 9th point at center of long side (see below).

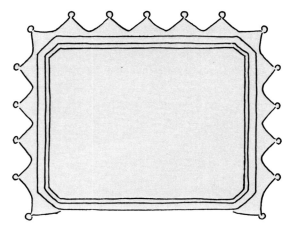

Attach border to three sides of cushion.

With WS together, stitch through both cushion pieces and pointed border close to edge.

◆

PENDANT

(Make 2.)

First, make a twisted cord with 3 33-inch (85cm) lengths of CC yarn (see Techniques). Leave folded end free. Make a knot approx 1 inch (3cm) from other end.

Each pendant consists of 4 balls and a ring at each end of an "acorn" threaded on the cord (see below).

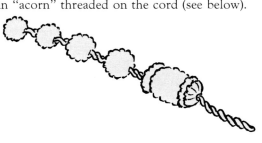

Pendant with 4 balls, 2 rings, and acorn

Each ball and space between increases in size. Use MC yarn for pendants.

Ball 1 (smallest hook)
Wind yarn twice around small finger.
Round 1: Work 5 (clear) sc into circle. Close hole. Sew end to secure.
Round 2: 2sc into each st to end.
Rounds 3–5: Sc to end.
Break yarn, leaving 5-inch (12cm) end. Weave end through sts of last round. Stuff ball, place cord knot inside, and pull yarn end to gather top. Secure with a few stitches.

Ball 2 (medium-size hook)
Follow instructions for Ball 1, but only partially close base hole. Thread onto cord, close, and sew base hole, leaving approx ¼ inch (5mm) space between balls. Stuff, gather, and secure.

Ball 3 (medium-size hook)
As Ball 2, but work 6sc into circle instead of 5sc. Thread onto cord, leaving ½ inch (1cm) space.

Ball 4 (medium-size hook)
Start as Ball 2, but work 7sc into circle.
Rep Rnds 2, 3, and 4.
Round 5: *sc2tog.
Rep from * to end.
Thread onto cord. Tighten base and secure. Add another sc round. Stuff, gather, and secure.

Ring (medium-size hook)
Make 2: Ch 8. Join with sl st into circle.
Round 1: 15sc into circle. Sew in end.
Work 2 more rounds of longer sc into circle, to cover 1st round, with 1sl st at end.

Acorn (medium-size hook)
Start as Ball 2, but work 7sc into circle.
Rep Rnd 2. Work 5sc rounds.
Round 8: *sc2tog.
Rep from * to end.
Thread onto cord with RS of rings touching each end of acorn. Stuff acorn, tighten, and secure ends. Sew final round of rings to acorn.
Sew folded pendant ends to inside of cushion at each side of opening.
Insert shaped pad. Close opening with overcasting, using either color of yarn.

Toilet Tissue Cover (page 82); Bathmat (page 82);
Filet Guest Towel Edgings (page 83).

CHAPTER SIX

The Bathroom

TOILET TISSUE COVER

A pretty nylon yarn makes this cover, which is simply a straight piece of striped crochet with ends joined to form a tube. Circles with a central tassel complete the top.

MATERIALS

111 yards (100m) of worsted-weight knitting ribbon in each of colors A and B (yarn shown: Sirdar DK Ribbon)
Size J/10 (6.00mm) hook
Matching sewing thread and needle

GAUGE

21sc = side width of 4¼ inches (11cm)

SIDE

With col A, ch 22 for a 4¼-inch- (11cm-) tall roll of toilet tissue.
(Make more or fewer ch as required.)
Row 1: (WS) 1sc into 2nd ch from hook, 1sc into next and each foll ch to end, turn.
Row 2: (Col B) Ch 2 (1st st). Into back loops only, 1sc into next and each foll st to end, turn.
Completing 2 rows of each color (Row 3, using col B), rep Row 2 until length equals circumference of toilet tissue. End with col B. Break yarn and fasten off. Join edges to form tube.

TOP

With col A, ch 4. Join with sl st into circle.
Round 1: Ch 1, 8sc into circle, sl st into 1st sc.
Round 2: Ch 2 (1st st), 1sc into same place, 2sc into next and each foll st to end.
With col B, sl st into top of 2ch. (16sts.)
Change color with sl st after every 2 rounds and complete a sc circle (increasing as necessary) to fit top of toilet tissue. End with sl st. Break off 1 color.

JOINING TOP TO SIDE

With yarn-change loops uppermost, pin edges together evenly, with RS of tube facing RS of circle. Work 1sc into each st from WS of circle. Break yarn and fasten off. Sew in ends securely. Turn RS out.

TASSEL

Cut 8 16-inch (40cm) lengths of either color of the ribbon and knot together at center. Feed knot through center hole and secure well on WS with a few sts. Trim ends.

BATHMAT

The wavy pattern for this mat, crocheted in a cotton yarn for water absorption and easy laundering, is made with increases and decreases at given points along each row.

MATERIALS

740 yards (700m) of a knitting worsted-weight cotton yarn in each of colors A and B
Size K/10½ (7.00mm) hook
Tapestry needle

GAUGE

With yarn trebled, 9dc = 4 inches (10cm) across

MEASUREMENTS

Excluding fringe, 21 × 26 inches (53 × 66cm)

INSTRUCTIONS

Use yarn tripled.
Leaving approx 5 inches (12cm) yarn at beg and end of each row, with col A, ch 64 fairly loosely (or any no. divisible by 10 plus 4).
Change yarn color during final stage of last dc of each row.
Row 1: (RS) With same col yarn, work 1dc into 4th ch from hook, *1dc into each of next 3ch,

82

dc3tog (over next 3ch), 1dc into each of next 3ch, 3dc into next ch. Rep from * to end. Work only 2dc into end ch. Turn.

Row 2: Ch 3 (1st st), 1dc into 1st st (last dc of prev row), *1dc into each of next 3sts, dc3tog, 1dc into each of next 3sts, 3dc into next st.

Rep from * to end. Work only 2dc into end st. Turn.

Rep last row 21 times more, or to required length of odd no. of rows, ending with col A.

Break yarn and fasten off.

With RS facing, join col A to beg of last row and ch 2. Working into front top loops only, 1sc into 1st st, *1sc into each of next 3sts, sc3tog, 1sc into each of next 3sts, sc3 into next st.

Rep from * to end. Work only 2sc into end st. Break yarn and fasten off.

With RS facing, join col A to beg of opp side (base ch). Ch 2, 1sc into each of next 4sts, 3sc into next st, *1sc into each of next 3sts, sc3tog (loosely), 1sc into each of next 3sts, 3sc into next st.

Rep from * to last 6sts, 1sc into each of next 4sts, sc2tog.

Break yarn and fasten off.

Using col B and tapestry needle, work running stitch between last 2 rows of completed long sides.

◆

FRINGE

Thread additional 5-inch (12cm) lengths of trebled yarn between existing ends so that there are 6 strands together at about ½-inch (1–1.5cm) intervals.

Using square knots, secure by knotting pairs of 3 strands together, close to rug. Trim.

FILET GUEST TOWEL EDGING
✳ ✳

This decorative pointed edging is worked in filet with lacets incorporated into the pattern to add a hint of elegance.

◆

MATERIALS

400 yards (370m) of a size 20 crochet cotton
(yarn shown: DMC Cebelia No. 20)
Size 8 steel (1.25mm) hook

◆

GAUGE/MEASUREMENTS

(Without ch edging) Width 1¾ × 3¼ inches
(4.8 × 8cm) at narrowest and widest points
12-row patt = 2½ inches (6cm)

◆

FILET

Sp = 1dc, 2ch, 1dc. Change the 2ch to 2dc to form a block of 4dc. (Last st of sq counts as 1st st of next sq.) Lacet = ch 3, 1sc, ch 3; bar = ch 5. For further instructions on filet crochet, see p. 11.

◆

INSTRUCTIONS

Ch 27.

Row 1: 1dc into 4th ch from hook, 1dc into each of next 2ch—1st block made, (ch 2, skip next 2ch, 1dc into next ch) 4 times, ch 3, skip next 2ch, 1sc into next ch, ch 3, skip next 2ch, 1dc into each of next 4ch, turn.

Row 2: Ch 3 (1st st), 1dc into each of next 3dc, ch 5, skip lacet, 1dc into next dc, complete 4sps and 1 block, turn.

Row 3: Ch 5, 1dc into 4th dc, for 1st sp. Work 4 more sps, closing last sp with 1dc. Work 2dc into 1st half of next sp, 1dc into 3rd of 5ch, ch 3, skip next 2ch of 5ch bar, 1sc into next 3ch, skip next 2dc, 1dc into end dc, inc 1 block at end of this row, turn.

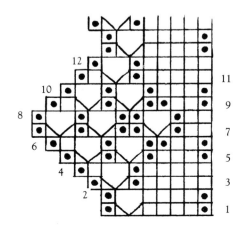

The filet edgings add a hint of elegance to your towels.

RIGHT: *Small Curtain (this page); Lavender Sachets (page 86); Tissue Box Covers (page 87).*

Cont from Row 4–12, then rep Rows 1–12 following chart on page 83 to required length, but work Rows 1 and 2 once more at end.

•

OUTER EDGING

(See below.)

Along pointed edge, starting at end of 1st row, work 1sc into each block (outer) corner, linking each sc with 4ch. Around the 2 blocks at each tip, work (ch 4, 1dc between 2 blocks, ch 4), and (ch 4, 1sc, ch 4) between points.

Hand- or machine-stitch edging either to edge of towel or a few inches in from edge.

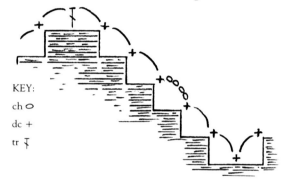

KEY:
ch ○
dc +
tr ⌇

Outer edging, showing positions of stitches and linking chains

SMALL CURTAIN

A small openwork arch design forms the pattern for this curtain. Loops and a fringe of crochet complete the top and base. Make to fit width of window, or slightly wider for gentle gathering.

•

MATERIALS

400 yards (365m) of a size 10 crochet cotton
(yarn shown: DMC Cordonnet Spécial)
Size 7 steel (1.50mm) hook
Sewing needle

•

GAUGE

16 rows and 44 sts over patt = 4 inches (10cm) sq

•

MEASUREMENTS

(With heading and base fringe)
18 × 16 inches (45 × 40cm)
Length of heading and fringe:
1¼ inches (3cm) and 1 inch (2.5cm)

•

INSTRUCTIONS

Ch 169 (or any no. divisible by 20 plus 9).
Row 1: 1dc into 4th ch from hook, *ch 5, skip next 3 base ch, 1dc into each of next 2 base ch.
Rep from * to end, turn.
Row 2: Ch 3 (1st dc), 1dc into next dc, *ch 1, 1sc into next 5ch sp, ch 1, 1dc into each of next 2dc.
Rep from * to end, turn.

Row 3: Ch 3 (1st dc), 1dc into next dc, *ch 5, 1dc into each of next 2dc.
Rep from * to end, turn.
Rep last two rows until work measures approx 16 inches (40cm) (or desired length). Work Row 2 again.

◆

HEADING

Row 1: Ch 3 (1st dc), 1dc into next dc, ch 5, 1dc into each of next 2dc, turn.
Row 2: Ch 3 (1st, dc), 1dc into next dc, ch 1, 1sc into 5ch sp, ch 1, 1dc into each of next 2dc, turn. (7sts.)
Rep last two rows 4 times more. Break yarn and fasten off leaving approx 6 inches (15cm) for stitching.

*Skip next 13sts (3 holes) of final row before start of heading, join yarn, and work last 10 rows again, over next 7 sts.
Rep from * across curtain top.
Fold back each piece and, with same yarn, sew to final row before start of heading, to form loops.

◆

BASE

Working along base ch, join yarn to corner dc, and rep Rows 1 and 2 of heading, twice. Join yarn to next dc (5th from corner), and work the 4 rows again.
Rep across curtain base. Sew in all ends.

LAVENDER SACHETS

✳✳

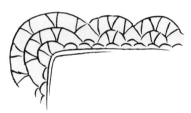

Sketch to show pattern for square sachet

These lavender sachets are made after completion of the pretty crocheted edging. Display them in a pretty bowl or basket, or slip them between towels and bed linen.

◆

MATERIALS

175 yards (160m) of a size 20 crochet cotton
(yarn shown: Twilleys 20)
Size 8 steel (1.25mm) hook
Small pieces of any suitable fabric
Sewing thread and needle
Lavender

◆

GAUGE/MEASUREMENTS

Inner and outer sqs = 3 inches and 4½ inches
(8cm and 12cm)
Inner and outer dias = 3½ inches and 5½ inches
(9cm and 14.5cm)

◆

SQUARE EDGING

Ch 104. Join with sl st into circle.
Round 1: Ch 1 (1st sc), 1sc into each of next 21ch, (3sc into next ch, 1sc into each of next 25ch) 3 times, 3sc into next ch, 1sc into each of next 3ch, sl st into 1st sc.
Round 2: Ch 1 (1st sc), 1sc into each of next 22sc, (3sc into next corner sc, 1sc into each of next 27sc) 3 times, 3sc into next corner sc, 1sc into each of next 4sc, sl st into 1st sc.
Round 3: *Ch 2, skip next sc, (1sc into next sc, ch 2, skip next sc) to next corner, (1dc, ch 1, 1dc) into corner sc.
Rep from * 3 times more, (ch 2, skip next sc, 1sc into next sc) twice, ch 2, 1sc into 1st 2ch sp.
Round 4: *{[ch 2, (1dc, ch 1, 1dc) into next sp, (ch 2, 1sc) into each of next 2sps]} 3 times, ch 2, skip next sp, (1dc, ch 1, 1dc) into next 2ch sp, ch 2, (1dc, ch 1, 1dc) into 1ch corner sp, ch 2, (1dc, ch 1, 1dc) into next 2ch sp, skip next sp, (ch 2, 1sc) into each of next 2sps.
Rep from * to end, but work the final (ch 2, 1sc) into only 1sp at end of round.
Ch 2.
Round 5: [(1dc, ch 1, 1dc) into next 2ch sp, ch 2, (1dc, ch 1, 1dc) into next 1ch sp, ch 2, (1dc, ch 1, 1dc) into next 2ch sp, skip next sp] 3 times.
Around corner, work (1dc, ch 1, 1dc) into next 2ch sp, ch 2, [(1dc, ch 1, 1dc) into next 1ch sp, ch 2, skip 2ch] twice, (1dc, ch 1, 1dc) into next 1ch sp, ch 2, (1dc, ch 1, 1dc) into next 2ch sp, skip next sp.
Rep from * to end, sl st into top of 1st dc.

ROUND EDGING

Ch 88. Join with sl st into circle.

Round 1: Ch 1 (1st sc), 1sc into each foll ch to end, sl st into 1st sc.

Round 2: *Ch 2, 1sc into next sc.
Rep from * to end, but working last sc into 1st sp on Rnds 2–7.

Rounds 3–6: *Ch 3, 1sc into next sp.
Rep from * to end.

Round 7: As Rnd 3 but ch 4 instead of ch 3.

Round 8: Ch 3, *(3sc, ch 1, 3sc) into next sp.
Rep from * working (2sc, ch 1, 2sc) into 1st sp at end of round. Sl st into next sc.

Cut 2 fabric squares or circles ½ inch (1cm) larger all around than inner edge of crochet edging. Sew up lavender bag, enclosing crochet edging in narrow seam. Leave a small opening.

Fill with dried lavender flowers. Do not pack too tightly. Close opening.

TISSUE BOX COVER

✳✳

Making a pretty cover for a tissue box means that a necessary, but not always very decorative, item can be kept on hand in the bathroom all the time.

MATERIALS

223 yards (204m) of a sport-weight cotton (yarn shown: Sirdar 4 ply Soft Cotton)

Size D/3 (3.00mm) hook

Piece of medium-weight fabric, box-top size plus ¾ inch (2cm) all around. (A lighter fabric can be used double or together with a lining fabric.)

½ inch- (1cm-) wide tape or ribbon to fit around oval and box top

Matching sewing thread and needle

GAUGE

20hdc = 4 inches (10cm) across

INSTRUCTIONS

Fit fabric onto box. Mark and cut oval from fabric center, approx ½ inch (1cm) smaller all around than box oval. Snip edge, turn under to WS, and baste in place. (If using doubled fabric, baste raw edges between fabrics.) Finished fabric oval should be very slightly smaller than box oval.

Using the crochet yarn, sew an oval of fairly loose ¼ inch- (5mm-) long sts, ¼ inch (5mm) apart, close to fold. Remove basting.

Working away from center, insert hook into any st and join yarn.

Round 1: Ch 2, *1sl st into next st, ch 2.
Rep from * to end.

Round 2: Into each 2ch sp, (1sc, 1hdc, 1dc, 1hdc, 1sc). Break yarn and fasten off. Sew in ends.

If using single fabric, sew tape to WS to cover raw edge of oval. Trim fabric to fit box top plus ½ inch (1cm) all around. Back-stitch ¼ inch- (5mm-) long sts, ½ inch (1cm) from outer edge. Opp sides should have equal no. of sts. Working away from fabric, join yarn to any st at corner.

Round 1: Ch 2 (1st hdc), 1hdc into next and each foll st to end, sl st into top of 2ch.

Cont with rounds of hdc until work reaches base of box. Break yarn and fasten off.

TRIMMING

Make a ch (with no. of sts divisible by 3 – 1) to fit around outside of box.

(Each row is worked from the same end.)

Row 1: (RS) 1sc into 2nd ch from hook, 1sc into each foll ch to end. Break yarn and fasten off.

Row 2: Rejoin to 1st st of Row 1.
Ch 1, 1sc into next sc, *ch 2, skip next sc, 1sc into each of next 2sc. Rep from * omitting 1sc at end. Break yarn and fasten off.

Row 3: Rejoin to 1st 2ch sp.
Ch 1, (1hdc, 1dc, 1hdc, 1sc) into same sp, (1sc, 1hdc, 1dc, 1hdc, 1sc) into each foll 2ch sp to end. Break yarn and fasten off.

Beg at opp end from slipknot, sew trimming to 3rd round from cover edge. Attach tape or ribbon to cover rem raw edge of fabric.

Bassinette Canopy and Ruffle (page 90); Filet Bassinette Trim (page 90).

CHAPTER SEVEN
The Nursery

FILET BASSINETTE TRIM

✸✸

Decorated with butterflies perched on flowers, this ruffle, worked in the finest cotton filet crochet, is sure to be treasured as an heirloom. The instructions allow you to make it to fit exactly.

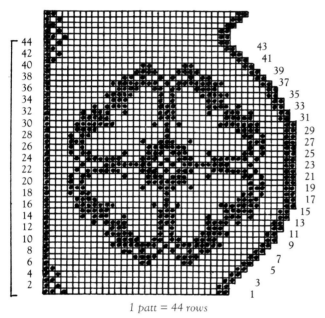

1 patt = 44 rows

MATERIALS

A size 20 crochet cotton (yarn shown: DMC Cebelia No. 20)
800 yards (740m) = approx 40 inches (1m) length
Size 8 steel (1.25mm) hook

GAUGE/MEASUREMENTS

6 inches (15cm) and 8½ inches (22cm) deep (shortest and longest points)
8¼ inches (21.5cm) = 1 pattern of 44 rows

FILET

Sp = 1dc, ch 2, 1dc. Change the ch2 to 2dc to form a block of 4dc. (Last st of sq counts as 1st st of next sq.) For further instructions on filet crochet, see p. 11.

INSTRUCTIONS

Ch 96.
Row 1: 1dc into 4th ch from hook, 1dc into each of next 5ch, *ch 2, skip next 2ch, 1dc into nest ch. Rep from * to last 12ch, 1dc into each of next 3ch, ch 2, skip next 2ch, 1dc into each of next 7ch, turn. Follow chart from Row 2, shaping as shown. Patt repeats after Row 44.

CANOPY AND RUFFLE

✸✸✸

You will need to measure up your bassinette before you decide what size to make your canopy, but the channel at the top will make it easy to fit on. The canopy edging and deep ruffle are made from individual motifs which you can work a few at a time.

MATERIALS

1,760 yards (1,620m) of a size 20 crochet cotton (yarn shown: Coats Crochet Cotton No. 20)

Size 8 steel (1.25mm) hook
2 yards (1.8m) of 44 inch- (114cm-) wide cotton fabric (selveges are at top and base of canopy, so any pattern on the fabric should be acceptable this way around)
Sewing thread and needle

GAUGE

Work to complete 1 motif to equal approx 3¼ inch (8.5cm) dia, measured from center corners

MEASUREMENTS

Length, including ruffle = 50 inches (127cm)
Width, including edging = 67 inches (170cm)
edge to edge
Make approx 129 motifs for the ruffle:
440 yards (405m) of crochet cotton will
complete approx 14 motifs.

MOTIF

Ch 23, fairly tightly.

Row 1: (Filet) 1dc into 8th ch from hook (2ch + dc + 2ch), *ch 2, skip next 2ch, 1dc into next ch.
Rep from * to end, turn. (6sqs.)

Row 2: Ch 5 (tr + 2ch), skip 1st 2ch, 1dc into next dc, *ch 2, skip next 2ch, 1dc into next dc.
Rep from * to end, turn.
Rep last row until 6 × 6 filet sqs.
Do not turn. Work around 4 sides as follows:

Round 1: 1sl st into same corner sq, ch 5 (tr + ch). Into same sp work (1tr, ch 1) 3 times. *Along next side, skip next sq, 1sc into next sp, ch 5, 1sc into next sp, ch 1, skip next sq, (1tr, ch 1) 11 times into next corner sp.
Rep from * but into final corner sq work (1tr, ch 1) only 7 times. Sl st to 4th of 1st 5ch.

Round 2: 1sl st into next 1ch sp, ch 7 (tr + 3ch), 1tr into next 1ch sp, ch 3, 1tr into next sp, *ch 1 (skip sp between 11th of same tr grp and filet), 1sc into next 5ch sp, ch 1, (skip sp between filet and next tr), 1tr into next sp, (ch 3, 1tr) into each of next 9sps.
Rep from * along rem sides but into 1ch sps of final corner work (1tr, ch 3) only 7 times. Sl st to 4th of 7ch.
The ruffle consists of 43 motifs wide ý 3 motifs deep, although once gathered, the number across may need to be adjusted. With sewing thread join motifs together on WS by stitching over and through the 3ch sts that link the 3rd to 4th tr and 7th to 8th tr of a corner.

CANOPY

1 Cut off a 1 inch- (2.5cm-) wide ribbon from one raw edge of fabric and leave to one side.
2 Make a ½ inch- (1cm-) wide double hem along each raw edge of main fabric.
3 Fold in half, hems together along one side. Make a 6 inch- (15cm-) long cut for an opening at one end of fold (top).

4 Using a length of the ribbon, bind around the opening.
5 Baste a single hem along base.
6 Join halves together at the top by first pressing 1¼ inch (3cm) of fabric along rem selvage edges to WS. Fold canopy down center. WS together, and make one line of stitching across the top through 4 layers (and hems), fairly close to selvage edges.
7 Make a parallel line of stitching through 2 layers to form a ¾–1 inch- (2–2.5cm-) wide channel.

GATHERING RUFFLE

(See below.)

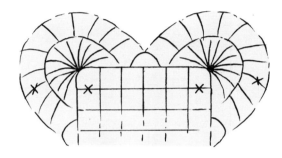

The four crosses indicate sc positions on one motif for gathering the ruffle

Row 1: Using hook and crochet cotton, work on WS along uppermost row of filet sqs.
Insert hook under base and into sp of 1st corner sq, join yarn and ch 2. Skip next 4sqs along, 1sc under base and into next corner sp. Ch 2, 1sc around stem of 3rd tr (2nd rnd) of same motif, ch 2, 1sc around stem of corresponding tr of next motif, ch 2, 1sc under base and into next corner sq of 2nd motif.
Continue along ruffle, working (1sc, ch 2) 4 times into each motif. Omit final 2ch, and do not work into last tr. Turn.

Row 2: Ch 3 (dc), 4dc into 1st 2ch sp, 5dc into each foll 2ch sp to end.
Attach dc row of ruffle to RS of canopy, completing base hem—allow 2 tr rounds to extend over sides on the 3 motifs at each end.

EDGING FOR FRONT OPENING

Make 2 filet ribbons, each the full length of canopy, excluding ruffle. Work as filet center of motif, but with only 14ch instead of 23ch. (3sqs.) Rejoin yarn to center sq at one end of a ribbon.

Row 1: Ch 1. Into next corner sp work (1tr, ch 1) 12 times (ribbon top).

Working along side, skip next sq, 1sc into next sp, ch 5, 1sc into next sp, *ch 1, skip next sq, (1tr, ch 1) 6 times into next sp, skip next sq, 1sc into next sp, ch 5, 1sc into next sp.

Rep from * to end of side, leaving last few sqs unworked for tucking under top corner of ruffle. Break yarn and fasten off. With RS facing, rejoin to unworked corner sp at opp end of ribbon.

Row 2: Ch 3, 1tr into sp between 1st 2tr, (ch 3, 1tr) into each of next 10sps, ch 1, 1sc into next 5ch sp, *ch 1, 1tr into sp between next 2tr, (ch 3, 1tr) into each of next 4sps, ch 1, 1sc into next 5ch sp. Rep from * to end.

For the 2nd ribbon, leave the same number of sqs unworked as on 1st ribbon, join yarn to next sq and ch 5, 1sc into next sp, ch 1, skip next sq, *(1tr, ch 1) 6 times into next sp, miss next sq, 1sc into next sp, ch 5, 1sc into next sp, ch 1, skip next sq. Rep from * to last sq, (1tr, ch 1) 12 times into corner sp, 1sc into center sq at end of ribbon.

Complete 2nd row from opp end, matching 1st ribbon.

Note the RS of each ribbon.

Pin the 3-sq width of each ribbon to RS of fabric at edges of opening, allowing the 2tr rows to extend over sides.

Sew to canopy.

DRESS

A sweet little dress, surprisingly simple to make, and equally suitable for that special baby girl.

♦

MATERIALS

380 yards (350m) of a baby yarn (yarn shown: Sirdar Snuggly 3 ply)
Size D/3 (3.00mm) hook
1 yard (1m) narrow eyelet lace
2 small buttons
Tapestry and sewing needles

♦

GAUGE

23dc and 17 rows = 4 inches (10cm) sq
Over loop patt, 10sc + 9 loops and
26 rows = 4 inches (10cm) sq

MEASUREMENTS

Length = 12½ inches (32cm)
Bodice width = 7 inches (18cm)
Skirt width = 13 inches (34cm)
Sleeve length = 2 inches (5cm)

♦

SKIRT

Beg at skirt top, ch 104.
Row 1: 1sc into 6th ch from hook, *ch 3, skip next ch, 1sc into next ch. Rep from * to end, turn.

Row 2: Ch 3, 1sc into 1st loop, (ch 3, 1sc) into each of next 2 loops, *inc 1 loop by working ch 2, 1sc into same loop as last sc, (ch 3, 1sc) into each of next 3 loops.

Rep from * working into only 2 loops at end, turn.

Row 3: Ch 3, 1sc into 1st loop, *ch 3, 1sc into next loop. Rep from * to end, turn.

Rep last row 15 times more. Omit (ch 3, 1sc) into last loop of final row (for underlay).

Cont loop patt (with the one less loop) until 9 inches (23cm) from base ch.

Break yarn and fasten off.

♦

FRONT BODICE

Row 1: Working over center 20 loops of skirt top (underlay on lhs), join yarn and ch 2 into 1st of 20 loops (1st st), 1sc into same loop, 2sc into each of next 19 loops. (Mark as RS.) Turn.

Row 2: Ch 3 (1st st), dc2tog (over next 2sc), 1dc into each foll st to last 3sts, dc2tog, 1dc into lst st, turn. (38sts.)

Row 3: Ch 1 (1st st), 1sc into each foll st to end, turn.

Row 4: Ch 3 (1st st), 1sc into each foll st to end, turn.

Row 5–11: Rep Rows 3 and 4, 3 times more, and Row 3 again.

Baby Jacket (page 94)

RIGHT NECK

Row 1: Ch 3 (1st st), 2dc into next st, 1dc into each of next 6sts, dc2tog, 1dc into next st. (Mark 17th sc from last dc made, for beg of left neck.) Turn.
Rows 2 and 3: Ch 1 (1st st), work 10sc to end, turn. Break yarn and fasten off.

LEFT NECK

Row 1: With WS facing, rejoin yarn to marked st. Ch 3 (1st st), dc2tog, 1dc into each of next 6sts, 2dc into next st, 1dc into last st, turn.
Rows 2 and 3: Ch 1 (1st st), work 10sc to end, turn. Break yarn and fasten off.

RIGHT BACK BODICE

Row 1: With RS facing, join yarn to 5th loop (skirt top) from left edge of front bodice. Ch 2 (1st st), 1sc into same loop, 2sc into each of next 10 loops, turn.
Row 2: Ch 3 (1st st), 1dc into each foll st to last 3 sts, dc2tog, 1dc into last st, turn.
Row 3: Ch 1 (1st st), 1sc into each foll st to end, turn.
Row 4: Ch 3 (1st st), 1dc into each foll st to end, turn.
Rows 5–11: Rep Rows 3 and 4, 3 times more, and Row 3 again.

Row 12: Ch 3 (1st st), 1dc into each foll st to last 2sts, 2dc into next st, 1dc into last st, turn.
Row 13: As Row 3. Break yarn and fasten off.
Row 14: Turn WS out. Working toward armhole, rejoin yarn to 11th sc from armhole edge, and rep Row 3 once more. Break yarn and fasten off.

LEFT BACK BODICE

Row 1: With RS facing, join yarn to unworked end loop of skirt top. Ch 2 (1st st), 1sc into same loop, 2sc into each of next 10 loops, turn.
Row 2: Ch 3 (1st st), dc2tog, 1dc into each foll st to end, turn.
Row 3: Ch 1 (1st st), 1sc into each foll st to end, turn.
Row 4: Ch 3 (1st st), 1dc into each foll st to end, turn.
Rows 5–11: Rep Rows 3 and 4, 3 times more, and Row 3 again.
Rows 12: Ch 3 (1st st), 2dc into next st, 1dc into each foll st to end, turn.
Row 13: As Row 3.
Row 14: Ch 1 (1st st), 1sc into each of next 10sts. Break yarn and fasten off.
Join shoulders by overcasting on WS.

RIGHT SLEEVE

(Work around sc and dc sts of armhole.)

Row 1: With RS facing, join yarn (near underarm) to 1st sc row of right back bodice, *(ch 3, skip next dc row, 1sc into end of next sc row) 6 times, ch 3, 1sc between top 2 sc rows at center shoulder edge, ch 3, 1sc into end of next sc row, (ch 3, skip next dc row, 1sc into end of next sc row) 6 times, turn.

Row 2: Ch 3, 1sc into 1st loop, (ch 3, 1sc) into each foll loop to end. Ch 3, 1sc into same end loop, turn. (15 loops.)

Row 3: Ch 3, 1sc into 1st loop, (ch 3, 1sc) into each foll loop to end, turn.

Rows 4–9: Rep last row 6 times more. Do not turn at end of last row.

Row 10: Join sleeve into circle by working 1sc into 1st loop of row, Ch 3 (1st st), 1dc into same loop, 2dc into each foll loop to end, sl st into top of 3ch. Break yarn and fasten off.

LEFT SLEEVE

With RS facing, join yarn to 1st sc row of rem side of front bodice.

Rep from * on right sleeve.

UNDERLAY

Row 1: With RS facing, join yarn to corner sc at neck opening (skirt underlay side) and work down bodice edge as follows:

Ch 2 (1st st), (2sc between end 2dc of next dc row, 1sc into end sc of next row) 6 times, 1sc into 1st loop at top of skirt, turn.

Row 2: Skip 1st st, 1sc into each foll st to end. Break yarn and fasten off.

NECK

Row 1: With RS facing, join yarn to unworked corner st at neck opening, ch 3 (1st st), 1dc into each of next 10sc, work 6dc to front neck, 16dc across front neck, 6dc to back neck, 11dc to end, omitting underlay rows.

Break yarn and fasten off.

Join back of skirt from base to skirt underlay. Add 1 or 2 sts to secure underlay base on WS. Join sleeve sides, omitting the 1st 3 rows (underarm). Gather skirt slightly at underarms and sew gathered edges along remainder of opened-out sleeve sides.

Sew in all ends. Attach buttons to bodice underlay and trimming to skirt edge.

BABY JACKET

This is the perfect little jacket to keep baby nice and warm. Finish it with white or pastel ribbon, if you like.

MATERIALS

380 yards (350m) of a baby yarn (yarn shown: Sirdar Snuggly 3 ply)
Size D/3 (3.00mm) hook
20 inches (50cm) narrow eyelet lace for sleeves (optional)
2 small buttons
Matching sewing thread and needle

GAUGE

23dc and 17 rows = 4 inches (10cm) sq, over patt

MEASUREMENTS

Width = 9 inches (23cm)
Back length = 9 inches (23cm)

BACK

Ch 56.

Row 1: 1sc into 2nd ch from hook, 1sc into each foll ch to end, turn.

Row 2: Ch 3 (1st st), 1dc into each foll st to end, turn.

Row 3: Ch 1 (1st st), 1sc into each foll st to end, turn.

Rows 4–21: Rep last two rows 9 times more.

Row 22: As Row 2.

Row 23: Ch 2, 1sl st into each of 2nd and 3rd sts,

ch 2 (1st sc), 1sc into each foll st to last 2 sts, turn. (51sts.)

Row 24: Ch 3 (1st st), dc2tog, 1dc into each foll st to last 3sc, dc2tog, 1dc into last sc, turn.

Row 25: Ch 1 (1st st), sc2tog, 1sc into each foll st to last 3sts, sc2tog, 1sc into last st, turn.

Rep last two rows until 19sts. (Rows 26–39.)

Row 40: As Row 24. Break yarn and fasten off.

◆

LEFT FRONT

Ch 29.

Work Rows 1–22 as for back.

Row 23: Ch 1, 1sl st into each of 2nd and 3rd sts, ch 2 (1st sc), 1sc into each foll st to end, turn. (26sts.)

Row 24: Ch 3 (1st st), 1dc into each foll st to last 3sc, dc2tog, 1dc into last sc, turn.

Row 25: Ch 1 (1st st), sc2tog, 1sc into each foll st to end, turn.

Rows 26–31: Rep last two rows 3 times more.

Row 32: Ch 3 (1st st), dc2tog, 1dc into each foll st to last 3sts, dc2tog, 1dc into last st, turn.

Row 33: As Row 25. (15sts.)

Row 34–39: Rep last two rows 3 times more.

Row 40: Ch 3 (1st st), (dc2tog) twice, 1dc into last st. Break yarn and fasten off.

◆

RIGHT FRONT

Ch 29.

Work Rows 1–22 as for back.

Row 23: Ch 1 (1st st), 1sc into each foll st to last 2sts, turn. (26sts.)

Row 24: Ch 3 (1st st), dc2tog, 1dc into each foll st to end, turn.

Row 25: Ch 1 (1st st), 1sc into each foll st to last 3sts, sc2tog, 1sc into last st, turn.

Row 26–31: Rep last two rows 3 times more.

Row 32: Ch 3 (1st st), dc2tog, 1dc into each foll st to last 3sts, dc2tog, 1dc into last st, turn.

Row 33: As Row 25. (15sts.)

Rows 34–39: Rep last two rows 3 times more.

Row 40: Ch 3 (1st st), (dc2tog) twice, 1dc into last st. Break yarn and fasten off.

◆

SLEEVE

Ch 28, fairly loosely.

Row 1: 1sc into 2nd ch from hook, 1sc into each foll ch to end, turn.

Row 2: Ch 3 (1st st), 2dc into next st, 1dc into each foll st to last 2sts, 2dc into next st, 1dc into last st, turn.

Row 3: Ch 1 (1st st), 1sc into each foll st to end, turn.

Row 4: Ch 3 (1st st), 1dc into each foll st to end, turn.

Rows 5 and 6: Rep last two rows once more.

Row 7: As Row 3.

Row 8: As Row 2.

Rows 9–12: Rep Rows 3 and 4 twice more.

Row 13: As Row 3.

Row 14: As Row 2.

Rows 15–18: Rep Rows 3 and 4 twice more.

Row 19: As Row 3.

Row 20: As Row 2.

Row 21: Ch 1, 1sl st into each of 2nd and 3rd sets sts, ch 2 (1st sc), 1sc into each foll st to last 2sts, turn. (31sts.)

Row 22: Ch 3 (1st st), dc2tog, 1dc into each foll st to last 3sc, dc2tog, 1dc into last sc, turn.

Row 23: Ch 1 (1st st), 1sc into each foll st to end, turn.

Row 24: Ch 3 (1st st), dc2tog, 1dc into each foll st to last 3sts, dc2tog, 1dc into last st, turn.

Rep last two rows until 13sts. Break yarn and fasten off. Make another sleeve the same.

On WS, butt together raglan edges of front, sleeve, back, sleeve, front, and sew togehter in turn. (Either side of patt can be chosen as RS.) Sew sleeve and side seams.

◆

NECK

With WS facing, join yarn to top of 1st dc at opening edge of L front neck.

Row 1: Ch 1 (1st st), 1sc into each of next 3dc, work 7sc evenly across sleeve top, 17sc across back, 7sc evenly across 2nd sleeve top, 4sc along top of R front neck, turn.

Row 2: Skip 1st st, 1hdc into next st, 1dc into each st to last 2sts of row, decreasing 1 st at center back, 1hdc into next st, 1sl st into last st. Break yarn and fasten off.

With RS facing, join yarn to base st at opening edge of R front, work 3sc around end dc (stem) of each dc row up to neck, 1sc between skipped st and 1st hdc of neck, 1sc between hdc and next dc, 1sc into each dc around neck, to last hdc. Work 1sc between last dc and hdc, 1sc between hdc and sl st, 3sc around end dc (stem) of each dc row to base of L front. Break yarn and fasten off. Sew in ends. Attach buttons. Sew trimming to RS of sleeve edges and fold back, adding one or two sts to secure.

BONNET

✳ ✳

 This light, warm bonnet is perfect for the bonny baby in your life. The back is worked first from base to top, then the sides are added in one piece. Complete the picture with a small ruffle around the face and neck edges.

◆

MATERIALS

190 yards (175m) of a baby yarn (yarn shown:
Sirdar Snuggly 3 ply)
Size D/3 (3.00mm) hook
⅞ yard (80cm) of 1 inch- (2.5cm-) wide ribbon
Matching sewing thread and needle

◆

GAUGE

23dc and 17 rows = 4 inches (10cm) sq
Over loop patt, 10dc + 9 loops and
26 rows = 4 inches (10cm) sq

◆

MEASUREMENTS

Face edge = 13 inches (33cm)
Back length = 5¼ × 5¼ inches (13 × 13cm) widest part

◆

BACK

Ch 21.
Row 1: 1dc into 4th ch from hook, 1dc into each foll ch to end, turn.
Row 2: Ch 1 (1st sc), 2sc into next st, (1sc into each of next 7sts, 2sc into next st) twice, 1sc, turn.
Row 3: Ch 3 (1st dc), 1dc into each foll st to end, turn.
Row 4: Ch 1 (1st sc), 2sc into next st, 1sc into each of next 7sts, 2sc into next st, 1sc into each of next 2sts, 2sc into next st, 1sc into each of next 7 sts, 2sc into next st, 1sc, turn.
Row 5: As Row 3.
Row 6: Ch 1 (1st sc), 2sc into next st, 1sc into each of next 8sts, 2sc into next st, 1sc into each of next 4sts, 2sc into next st, 1sc into each of next 8sts, 2sc into next st, 1sc, turn.
Row 7: As Row 3.
Row 8: Ch 1 (1st sc), 1sc into each foll st to end, turn.
Row 9: As Row 3.
Rows 10 and 11: Rep last 2 rows once more.

Row 12: Ch 1 (1st sc), sc next 2sts tog, 1sc into each foll st to last 3sts, sc2tog, 1sc, turn.

Row 13: As Row 3.

Row 14: As Row 8.

Row 15: As Row 3.

Row 16: As Row 12.

Row 17: As Row 3.

Row 18: Ch 1 (1st sc), sc2tog, 1sc into each of next 4sts, sc2tog, 1sc into each of next 8sts, sc2tog, 1sc into each of next 4sts, sc2tog, 1sc, turn. (22sts.)

Row 19: As Row 3.

Row 20: Ch 1 (1st sc), sc2tog, (1sc into each of next 4sts, sc2tog) 3 times, 1sc, turn.

Row 21: Ch 2 (1st hdc), dc2tog, 1dc into each foll st to last 3sts, dc2tog, 1hdc, turn.

Row 22: Ch 1 (1st sc), sc2tog, (1sc into each of next 2sts, sc2tog) 3 times, 1sc. (12sts.)

Break yarn and fasten off.

◆

SIDE

Begin by working loops around edge of back, excluding base.

Row 1: With preferred side facing (RS), join yarn between 2 end dcs of 1st row.

Ch 3, 1sc into same sp, * (ch 3, 1sc) into each edge sp of next 5 dc rows, ch 3, (1sc, ch 3, 1sc = inc loop) into next dc row, (ch 3, 1sc) into each of next 2 dc rows, ch 3, inc loop in next dc row, ch 3, (1sc, ch 3) into next end hdc row.

Across top 12sts, work (1sc, ch 3) into 2nd, 5th, 8th, and 11th sts.

Cont along rem edge to base, matching 1st side, turn. (21 loops.)

Row 2: Ch 3, 1sc into 1st loop, *ch 3, 1sc into next loop. Rep from * to end, working one inc loop at center top, turn.

Rows 3–20: Omitting an inc, rep last row 18 times more (approx 2½ inches [7cm]).

Row 21: As patt, but work 2ch instead of 3ch loops, turn.

Row 22: Ch 2, 1sc into 1st loop, ch 2, *1sc into next sc, ch 2.

Rep from * to end, but work a sc into last 2ch loop, turn.

Rows 23 and 24: Work the (ch 3, 1sc) patt into each loop to end, turn.

Rows 25: As patt, but work 4ch instead of 3ch loops, turn.

Row 26: (WS facing) Ch 3, *(1sc, ch 3) 3 times into next loop. Rep from * to end, omitting final ch 3. Temporarily unhook loop. With RS facing, fold ruffle at Rows 21–22 (2ch rows) onto RS of bonnet. Reinsert hook and secure corner of ruffle in position by working a sl st at end of Row 16 (approx). Turn.

Row 27: (WS facing) Ch 2 (1st st), make 9sc evenly along neck edge of side, to base of back (working into the sps), 11sc evenly across base ch edge, picking up single sts of base ch, 10sc evenly into sps along neck edge of rem side until equivalent place is reached as at beg of this row. Fold ruffle onto RS, and attach corner with a sl st, as on prev row, turn.

Row 28: 1sc into last sc made, 1hdc into next sc, (ch 1, 1dc) twice into each foll sc to last 2sts, ch 1, 1hdc into next st, 1sl st into 2ch. Break yarn. Fasten off. Insert ribbon through each hole at end of ruffle, and sew securely in place.

BABY SHAWL
✳✳✳

A light, warm blanket with extra-frilly corners. A pattern of feathers and picot festoons combine to make a decorative border.

◆

MATERIALS

760 yards (700m) of a baby yarn (yarn shown: Sirdar Snuggly 3 ply)
Size D/3 (3.00mm) hook

◆

GAUGE

Over main section loop patt, 10sc + 9 loops and 26 rows = 4 inches (10cm) sq

◆

MEASUREMENTS

Main section = 27½ inches (70cm) sq
Border = Approx 4½ inches (12cm) deep

The Nursery

INSTRUCTIONS

Ch 134, loosely.

Row 1: 1sc into 4th ch from hook, *ch 3, skip next ch, 1sc into next ch.

Rep from * to end, turn. (66 loops.)

Row 2: Ch 3, 1sc into 1st loop, *ch 3, 1sc into next loop.

Rep from * to end, turn.

Rep last row until fabric is square. Turn.

BORDER

Round 1: 1st side—ch 7 (tr + 3ch), (1tr, ch 3) 5 times into 1st loop (corner), skip next loop, (1sc, ch 3) into each of next 2 loops, *skip next loop, (1tr, ch 3) 4 times into next loop, skip next loop, (1sc, ch3) into each of next 2 loops.

Rep from * to last 2 loops of side, skip next loop, (1tr, ch3) 6 times into next loop (corner).

(12 "fans" and 13 loops between corners.)

2nd side—(last corner loop = 1st row) 1sc into loop at edge of 5th row from 1st side, ch 3, 1sc into loop at edge of 7th row from 1st side, ch 3.

Cont by making a total of 12 fans and 13 loops evenly along 2nd side, to match 1st side, initially by pinning 1st side approx ¾ inch (2cm) below edge on front of 2nd side and following fan and loop positions.

After the final ch 3, work (1tr, ch 3) 6 times into last loop for corner.

3rd side—skip next loop, (1sc, ch3) into each of next 2 loops.

Rep from * as 1st side, completing foll corner.

4th side—work to match 2nd side. After final 3ch, sl st into 4th of 7ch.

Round 2: Sl st into next sp, ch 7 (tr + 3ch), (1tr, ch 3) twice and 1tr all into same sp, **(1tr, ch 3, 1tr = "V") into next sp, (1dtr, ch 3) 3 times and 1dtr all into next sp at center corner, "V" into next sp, (1tr, ch 3) 4 times into next sp.

Make a picot (= make 1dc, inserting hook through top loop and out of top left stem of last tr made). (Skip next tr, ch 3, sc), (1tr, ch 3) twice into next loop (of 13 loops), picot, *(1tr, ch 3) 4 times into next fan center loop, picot, (1tr, ch 3) twice into next loop (of 13 loops), picot.

Rep from * to next corner, (skip next sc, ch 3, tr), (1tr, ch 3) 3 times and 1tr all into 1st of next 5 corner sps.

Rep from **along rem sides to 1st corner, ending with picot. Sl st into 4th of 7ch.

Round 3: (Skipping next sp) work 5sl st into foll sp (= center of 1st fan of corner), ch 7 (1tr, ch 3) 3 times into same sp, **picot, (skip next tr, ch 3, 2tr), (1tr, ch 3) twice into next "V" sp, picot, (skip next tr, dtr, ch 3, dtr), work (1dtr, ch 3) 4 times into center sp of dtr fan at corner, picot (into dtr). (Skip next dtr, ch 3, dtr, tr), (1tr, ch 3) twice into next "V" sp, picot, *(1tr, ch 3) 4 times into center sp of next fan, picot, skip next sp, (1tr, ch 3) twice into "V" sp foll next picot, picot.

Rep from * to last picot of side, (1tr, ch 3) 4 times into center sp of tr fan at beg of corner.

Rep from ** along rem sides to beg of 1st corner, ending with picot. Sl st into 4th of 7ch.

Round 4: (Skipping next sp) work 5sl st into center sp of 1st fan of corner, ch 7, (1tr, ch 3) 3 times into same sp, **2 picots (= 1dc into last tr of dtr as before, ch 3, 1dc through top and side of last dc made), skip next sp and picot, (1tr, ch 3) twice into next "V" sp, 2 picots, (skip next picot and sp), work (1dtr, ch 3) 4 times into center sp of dtr fan at corner, 2 picots.

Skip next sp and picot, (1tr, ch 3) twice into next "V" sp, 2 picots, skip next picot and sp, *(1tr, ch 3) 4 times into center sp of next fan, picot, (1tr, ch 3) twice into "V" sp foll next picot, picot.

Rep from * to tr fan at beg of next corner, (1tr, ch 3) 4 times into center sp of fan.

Rep from ** along rem sides to beg of 1st corner, ending with picot.

Sl st into 4th of 7ch.

Round 5: Cont patt as Rnd 4 but instead of 2 picots in a row, work 3 picots.

Round 6: Cont patt as Rnd 4 but instead of 2 picots in a row, work 4 picots.

Round 7: (Skipping next sp), work 5sl st into center sp of 1st fan of corner, ch 7, 1dc into 4th ch from hook, (1tr, ch 3, picot) 5 times into same sp, **add 2 picots onto last picot, (1tr, ch 3, picot) 4 times into next "V" sp, 2 picots (= 3 in a row), (1dtr, ch 3, picot) 6 times into center corner sp, 2 picots.

Work (1tr, ch 3, picot) 4 times into next "V" sp, 2 picots, *(1tr, ch 3, picot) 6 times into next fan center, (1tr, ch 3, picot) 4 times into next "V" sp.

Rep from * to last single picot of side, (1tr, ch 3, picot) 6 times into next fan center.

Rep from ** along rem sides to 1st corner, sl st into 4th of 7ch.

Christmas Angel (page 106) with a variety of Christmas tree decorations (page 102-5).

CHAPTER EIGHT

Celebration

RIBBON

This looped ribbon, worked in glitter yarn, has many uses—including Christmas tree decorating, present wrapping, and holding Christmas cards—so make plenty!

MATERIALS

A fingering-weight glitter yarn (yarn shown: Twilleys Gold Dust)
Size 1 steel (2.00mm) and J/10 (6.00mm) hooks
Sewing needle

INSTRUCTIONS

To make approx 12 inches (30cm) of ribbon, double 3¼ yards (3m) of yarn. With larger hook, ch 45 (or any odd no.) with this doubled yarn.
Cont with smaller hook and single yarn from spool; ch 1.
Treat each ch st of doubled yarn as consisting of 6 strands, and insert hook so that 3 strands are above and 3 strands are below the hook.
Row 1: Into 2nd ch from hook, work 6hdc, *1sl st into next ch, 6hdc into foll ch.
Rep from * to end.
Row 2: With slipknot behind, work another 6hdc into same end ch.
Cont along opp side of ch length, repeating from * as for prev row, until end. Sl st into 1st st.
Sew in ends.

BELL

Simple single crochet, a small amount of embroidery, and a lovely glitter yarn all combine to make this little bell.

MATERIALS

Approx 20 yards (18m) of a fingering-weight glitter yarn (yarn shown: Twilleys Gold Dust)
Size B/1 (2.00mm) hook
Sewing needle

GAUGE

1st 4 rounds = 1 inch (2.5cm) dia

HEIGHT

2¼ inches (6cm)

INSTRUCTIONS

Leaving a 6-inch (15cm) end of yarn, ch 4. Join with sl st into circle.
Round 1: Ch 1, 8sc into circle, sl st into 1st sc.
Round 2: Ch 1 (1st sc), sc twice into each foll st to end, 1sc into st at base of 1st sc, sl st into 1st sc. (16sts.)

Round 3: Ch 1 (1st sc), 2sc into next st, *sc into next st, 2sc into foll st.
Rep from * to end, sl st into 1st sc.
Round 4: Work 24sl st to end.
Round 5: Ch 1 (1st sc), work 23 fairly loose sc under last round and between sc of Rnd 3, enclosing sl sts of Rnd 4. Sl st into 1st sc.
Round 6: Ch 1 (1st sc), sc to end, sl st into 1st sc. (24sts.)
Omit ch and sl st on foll rounds. Use marker to indicate round ends.
Round 7: Sc to end.
Round 8: Inc 1sc in 1st st, sc to end, working on outside.
Round 9: Sc to end, inc 1sc in 10th st.
Round 10: Sc to end, inc 1sc in 19th st.
Round 11 and 12: Sc to end.
Round 13: Sc to end, inc 1sc in 8th st.
Round 14: Sc to end, inc 1sc in 17th st.
Round 15: Sc to end, inc 1sc in 28th st.
Round 16: Sc to end, inc 1sc in every 5th st. (36sts.)
Round 17: Sc to end.

Round 18: Sc to end but inc 1sc in 3rd and every foll 6th st, ending with 3sc.
Round 19: Sc to end.
Round 20: Sc to end but skip 3rd and every foll 6th st, ending with 3sc. Work 1sl st to finish off. Break yarn. Fold final round to inside. Using the same yarn, overcast close upright sts over bell edge, and Rnd 5 at edge of top circle.

Wind yarn 6 times around finger. Tightly button-hole-st around this circle until firm.
Trim and fold double the 6-inch (15cm) end to fit inside for the "clapper." Double-knot one end and sew other end to inside. Sew on the handle, winding yarn a few times around handle base while stitching.

CHRISTMAS BALL

 Make this lovely 3-D decoration in metallic thread to hang where it will catch the light.

◆

MATERIALS

55 yards (50m) of a glitter yarn (yarn shown: Twilleys Goldfingering)
Size C/2 (2.50mm) hook
Sewing needle
Lightweight stuffing

◆

GAUGE

1st 5 rounds = 1½ inches (4cm) dia

◆

HEIGHT

Approx 2½ inches (6cm)

◆

INSTRUCTIONS

Ch 4. Join with sl st into circle.
Round 1: Work 8sc into circle.
Round 2: 2sc into each st.
Round 3: (1sc into next st, 2sc into foll st) 8 times.
Round 4: Sc to end.
Round 5: (1sc into each of next 5sts, 2sc into foll st) 4 times.
Round 6: (1sc into each of next 6sts, 2sc into foll st) 4 times.
Round 7: 1sc into each of next 3sts, 2sc into foll st, (1sc into each of next 7sts, 2sc into foll st) 3 times, 1sc into each of next 4sts. (36sts.)
Round 8: Sc to end.
Round 9: (1sc into each of next 8sts, 2sc into foll st) 4 times.
Rounds 10 and 11: Sc to end.
Round 12: Ch 10, skip next 10sts, sc to end.

Round 13: 1sc into each ch st, sc to end.
Round 14: Sc to end.
Round 15: (1sc into each of next 9sts, skip next st) 3 times, 1sc into each of next 8sts, skip next st, 1sc.
Round 16: Sc to end.
Round 17: 1sc into each of next 4sts, skip next st, (1sc into each of next 8sts, skip next st) 3 times, 1sc into each of next 4sts.
Round 18: (1sc into each of next 7sts, skip next st) 3 times, 1sc into each of next 6sts, skip next st, 1sc.
Round 19: (1sc into each of next 6sts, skip next st) 3 times, 1sc into each of next 5sts, skip next st, 1sc.
Round 20: (1sc into each of next 2sts, skip next st) 7 times, 1sc into next st, skip next st, 1sc.
Round 21: (1sc into each of next 4sts, skip next st) 3 times, 1sc.
Rounds 22–25: Sc to end.
Round 26: Sc to last st, 1sl st.
Leaving approx 12 inches (30cm) of thread, break yarn.
Fluff stuffing and fill loosely (see below). Close side opening. Fold final 2 rounds to inside top and with the same yarn sew across neck. Leave 8 inches (20cm) for loop. Decorate as desired.

To maintain the shape, the opening for stuffing is made at the side.

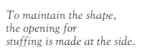

CHRISTMAS TREE DECORATIONS

These delightful little tree ornaments are quickly and easily made, and are ideal for finishing up scraps of yarn and other decorations. Try making a few for a pre-Christmas bazaar. They'll be snapped up!

◆

MATERIALS

Scraps of yarn (red and white for Boot, white cotton for Snow Crystal)
Hooks in suitable sizes
Beads, sequins, metallic thread, or other decorations
Cardboard (optional)
All-purpose glue
Fabric stiffener (optional)

◆

MEASUREMENTS

Depends on yarn and hook size. Heart in knitting worsted with a suitable hook size = approx 3 × 2½ inches (8 × 7cm)

◆

HEART ✳✳

Using main color (MC) yarn, ch 3. Join with sl st into circle.

Round 1: Ch 1, 7sc into circle, sl st into 1st sc. (7sts.)

Round 2: Ch 1 (1st st), 2sc into each of next 6sts, 1sc into sl st at base of 1st st, sl st into 1st st. (14sts.)

Round 3: Ch 2 (1st st), 4dc into next st, skip next st, 1sc into next st, skip next st, 4dc into next st, 1hdc into each of next 3sts, 3hdc into next st, 1dc into next st, 3hdc into next st, 1hdc into each of next 2sts, sl st into top of 2ch.

Round 4: Ch 1 (1st st), 1sc into each of next 2sts, (2hdc, 1dc) into next st, (1hdc, 1sc) into next st, 1sc into next st, (1sc, 1hdc) into next st, (1dc, 2hdc) into next st, 1sc into each of next 3sts, sc2tog, 1sc into each of next 4sts, ch 2, 1sc into each of next 5sts.
With contrasting color (CC) yarn, sl st into 1st st.

Round 5: Using same CC yarn, ch 2 (1st st), 1sc into each of next 3sts, 2sc into each of next 3sts, 1sc into next st, 1sl st into next st at center bow, 1sc into next st, 2sc into each of next 3sts, 1sc into each of next 9 sts, (1sc, ch 2, 1sc) into 2ch loop, 1sc into each of next 5sc.
With MC yarn, sl st into top of 1st 2ch.
Break off CC yarn.

Round 6: Ch 2, (1sl st into next st, ch 1) 9 times, 1sl st into next st, skip next sl st, (1sl st into next st, ch 1) 17 times, 1sl st into 2ch loop, ch 2, (1sl st into next sc, ch 1) 6 times, 1sl st into 1st of 2ch at start of round.
Fasten off.
Worked in a knitting worsted, the heart also makes a sweet pocket for a little girl's sweater.

◆

2-D BALL

Ch 6. Join with sl st into circle.

Round 1: Ch 3 (1st dc), 15dc into circle, sl st into top of 3ch.

Round 2: Ch 3 (1st dc), 1dc into same place as 3ch, 2dc into each of next 15dc, sl st into top of 3ch.

Round 3: Ch 3 (1st dc), 2dc into next st, *1dc into next st, 2dc into next st.
Rep from * to end, sl st into top of 3ch.

Round 4: Ch 1 (1st dc), 2dc to end, sl st into 1st sc.

Round 5: Ch 3 (1st dc), 2dc into each of next 2sts, 1dc into next st, turn.

Round 6: Ch 2 (1st sc), 5sc to end.
Fasten off.

◆

BOOT ✳

With white yarn, ch 15. Join with sl st into circle.

Round 1: (RS) Ch 3 (1st dc), 1dc into each foll ch to end, sl st into top of 3ch. (RS is outside.)

Round 2: Ch 2 (1st hdc), 1hdc into each foll st to end. Break off white yarn, sl st with red yarn into top of 2ch. (15hdc.)

Flatten work so that last sl st made (above 1st hdc) is on its own at rhs.

Row 1: Ch 1. Through both layers work 1sc into each of rem 7 hdc pairs, turn (see below).

Row 2: Ch 1 (1st sc), 1sc into each of next 6sts—leave last ch unworked, turn.

Work 1sc into each of seven pairs of stitches

Row 3: Ch 1 (1st sc), 6sc to end, turn.

Rep last row 3 times more.

Row 7: Ch 5. Into 2nd ch from hook, work 1sc, 3sc along remainder of ch, 1sc into each of next 7sts to end, turn.

Row 8: Ch 1 (1st sc), 1sc into each of next 6sts, sc2tog, sc to end, (10sc) turn.

Rows 9–11: Ch 1 (1st sc), sc to end, turn.

Row 12: 1sc into each of the 10sts—inc 1sc in last st. Do not turn. Cont around toe, 1sc into toe-side center, 1sl st into 5ch-end st of Row 7.

Break yarn and fasten off. Sew in ends.

Twist a length of red yarn and thread together, fold in half to form thin cord (see Techniques), and thread right around and between Rnds 1 and 2. Tie ends into a tiny bow.

◆

SNOW CRYSTAL ❋❋

Ch 6. Join with sl st into circle.

Round 1: Ch 3 (1st dc), work 23dc into circle, sl st into top of 3ch. (24dc.)

Round 2: *Ch3 (1st dc), 1dc into next st, ch 19, 1dc into each of next 2dc, ch 2.

Replace 1st 3ch with 1dc into next st, and rep from * to end, sl st into top of 3ch.

Round 3: *Working around next 19ch sts; ch 3, (1 sl st, ch 3, 1dc) into 3rd ch st, (1 sl st, ch 3, 2dc) into 6th ch st, 1sl st into 9th ch st, ch 2, 1hdc into 10th ch st, ch 2, 1sl st into 11th ch st, (2dc, ch 3, 1sl st) into 14th ch st, (1dc, ch 3, 1sl st) into 17th ch st, ch 3. (Skip both the remainder of 19ch and dc beneath), 1sl st into next dc, 1sl st into 1st of next 2ch, 1sl st into sp of same 2ch, ch 24.

Into 14th ch from hook, (1sl st, ch 15, 1sl st, ch 13, 1sl st). Work 10sl st along remainder of 24ch, 1sl st into 2nd of 2ch at base of 24ch just made, 1sl st into next dc. Rep from * to end, omitting last sl st at end of round. Fasten off. Press. Attach a sequin back and front at center and at 3-petal sl sts, and apply a fabric stiffener or glue, or sew to hexagonal cardboard with the sequins fixed to one side only (see below).

The crystal can either be stiffened, or mounted on a hexagonal piece of cardboard as shown

CHRISTMAS ANGEL

✳ ✳ ✳

This lovely angel is a must for the top of your Christmas tree. You will probably find the odds and ends of cloth and yarn you need to make her in your scrap basket. Note that she isn't suitable as a toy for small children.

◆
MATERIALS

283 yards (260m) of a size 10 crochet cotton in white (yarn shown: DMC Cebelia No. 10) (for wings, leg, and arm covering)
Size 7 steel (1.50mm) hook
Approx 17½ yards (16m) silver Lurex yarn (wings and decoration)
5 7-inch (18cm) lengths white wire—paper-clip strength (wings, dress hoop, halo, wand)
Any other color wire can be painted with white correction fluid.
All-purpose glue
1¼-inch- (3cm-) dia piece of eggshell and markers (face)
Gray or brown embroidery floss (leg division)
White sewing thread (dress and dress hoop)
8 × 13 inches (21 × 34cm) white sheeting (dress)
1-inch- (2.5cm-) thick sponge 4 × 7½ inches (10 × 19 cm) (body)
¾ inch (2cm) silver tinsel (wand star)
Small amount white sport-weight or knitting worsted yarn (hair)
Sewing needle
Optional:
Extras for dress decoration—sequins, beads, net

◆
HEIGHT

Approx 8 inches (20cm)

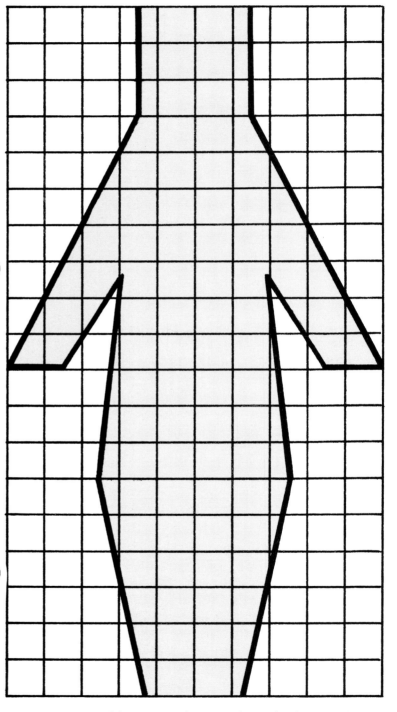

Cut out angel from a piece of sponge 4 × 7½ inches (10 × 19cm).

106

◆
INSTRUCTIONS

Make paper pattern from diagram on page 106. Cut out angel in sponge. Snip ⅛ inch (3mm) into sponge across tops of front and back legs. Trim off this ⅛ inch (3mm) excess sponge down to base, tapering slightly inward (see below left).

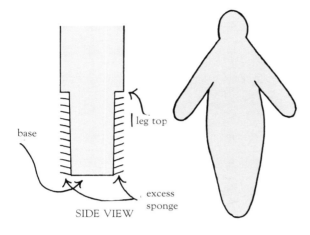

Trim away some sponge to distinguish the legs (left).
Completed body, after shaping (right)

Round of all edges, including corners of head top, tips of hands and feet, and trunk to legs.
Snip ½ inch (1cm) under arms, to lengthen (see above right).
(Front and back leg tops should each measure approx 1¾ inch [4.5cm] across.)

◆
LEG COVERING

(Feet to waist. Make 2.)
With crochet cotton, ch 38.
Row 1: 1sc into 2nd ch from hook, 1sc into each foll ch to end, turn.
Row 2: Ch 2 (count 2ch as 1st st of rows), 2sc into next st, 1sc into each foll st to end, turn. (38sts.)
Row 3: Ch 2, 1sc into each foll st to last 2sts, 2sc into next st, 1sc into last st, turn.
Rep last 2 rows once more.
Row 6: Ch 2, 1sc into each of next 21sts, 1hdc into each foll st to end, turn.
Row 7: Ch 2, 1hdc into each of next 19sts, 1sc into each foll st to end, turn.
Row 8: Ch 2, 1sc into each of next 20sts, 1hdc into each foll st to end, turn.
Row 9: Ch 2, 1sc into each foll st to end, turn.

Row 10: As Row 8.
Row 11: As Row 7.
Row 12: As Row 6.
Row 13: As Row 9.
Row 14: As Row 9, but dec 1 st at beg of row.
Row 15: As Row 9, but dec 1 st at end of row.
Rep last 2 rows once more. (37 sts.)
Break yarn and fasten off.
Leaving shorter straight edges open (waist), back-stitch curved ends tog, turn RS out, fit onto doll, and overcast sides tog. With 3 strands of embroidery floss, tightly stitch through leg coverings and sponge a dividing line for legs (see below). Separate feet slightly with a final overcast st.

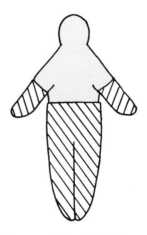

Cover angel's arms and legs. Divide legs with a line of stitches down the center

◆
ARM AND HAND COVERING

(Make 2.)
With crochet cotton, ch 16.
Row 1: 1sc into 2nd ch from hook, 1sc into each foll ch to end, turn.
Row 2: Ch 2 (count 2ch as 1st st of rows), 2sc into next st, 1sc into each foll st to end, turn. (16sts.)
Row 3: Ch 2, 1sc into each foll st to last 2sts, 2sc into next st, 1sc into last st, turn.
Row 4: As Row 2.
Row 5: Ch 2, 1hdc into each of next 8sts, 1sc into each foll st to end, turn.
Rows 6–13: Ch 2, 1sc into each foll st to end, turn.
Row 14: Ch 2, 1sc into each of next 8sts, 1hdc into each foll st to end, turn.
Row 15: As Row 6, but dec 1 st at end of row.
Row 16: As Row 6, but dec 1 st at beg of row.

Row 17: As Row 6, but dec 1 st at end of row.
Row 18: As Row 6. (15sts.)
Break yarn and fasten off.
Fold sides tog to form glove. Using the same yarn, back-stitch curved end, turn RS out, fit glove onto doll, and stitch sides (see page 107 right).

◆
DRESS

Form one piece of wire into a circle, overlapping ends by ½ inch (1cm). Place a dab of glue over ends and wind the sewing thread tightly around, to secure. Join together two short edges of sheeting with a flat-fell seam (see below).

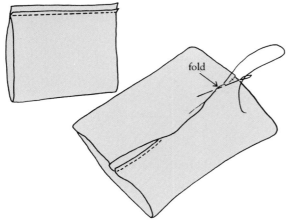

Make a tube from the fabric. Place one edge below the other to start a flat-fell seam. Fold over the deeper edge and stitch down

Turn ½ inch (1cm) of one raw edge (neck) to WS, and baste in place. Make a ⅓ inch (8mm) hem on RS with rem raw edge, enclosing hoop between two circles of small sts.
Place dress on doll with seam down the back and wire circle at base. Gather neck and secure. Remove basting. Adjust dress gathers evenly around body. With arms flat against body, cut two small horizontal slits in dress just above wrist fronts, to bring hands through. Stitch openings to wrists. Cover with small chains, as bracelets, made with the Lurex yarn. Separate sleeves from bodice with a few sts in cotton thread.
Lift hoop upward, outside dress, to hip level. Even out gathers. Squeeze together back and front of hoop and bend sides slightly upward. Glue or sew narrow waves of a Lurex chain around dress to conceal hoop stitching (see above right). Add extra dress decoration if desired.

Dressed doll

◆
FACE AND DECORATION

Form curls with knitting yarn wound over the end of a crochet hook, and carefully slide onto dabs of glue applied on head. Leave out curls nearest face until face is in position. Apply a little glue over completed curls to set, and shine, hair. Affix face (as close to a 1¼ inch [3cm] dia circle of eggshell as is possible) onto doll with glue, and position final curls. Add light features with markers.
Glue or sew on small Lurex chains for necklaces. Embroider a silver star onto point of each foot.

◆
WINGS

(Make 2.)
Join ends of a piece of wire, as on dress hoop, and shape as shown below. (If used, omit correction fluid for wings, as wire is concealed.)
Round 1: Using white crochet cotton, work 114 sc evenly around wire, leaving join until last. Sl st into 1st sc.

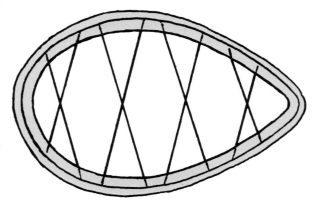

Wing shape, with crosses in silver yarn for decoration

Round 2: Change to silver yarn and work 1sc into every alternate st. Sl st into 1st sc.

Round 3: (White) 1sc into each st to end but inc 2sts at bend and inc 12 more sts evenly over round. Sl st into 1st sc.

Round 4: (Silver) Ch 5, skip next st, *1sc into next st, ch 4, skip next st.

Rep from * to end, sl st into 1st of 5ch. Break yarn and sew in ends.

Use silver yarn to decorate with crosses as shown on page 108. To stiffen, paint first two rounds and crosses, with 2 teaspoons of sugar dissolved in approx a teaspoon of boiling water. Allow to dry thoroughly.

Shape halo from another piece of wire (see right). Taking care not to damage face, push (slightly slanting to the back) through back curls, allowing end to rest at back of neck. Glue point of entry through curls. To make the wand (optional), fold wire in half at 4 inches (10cm) from one end. Twist, leaving a thin loop at fold. Glue tinsel through loop (see right). Sew onto hand. Sew wings into sponge, at center back of doll.

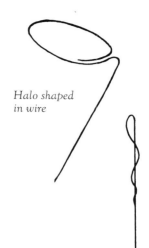

Halo shaped in wire

Wand showing loop for tinsel

SNOWMAN

Made all-in-one, this snowman has a detachable base which makes him easy to launder and keep snowy white.

MATERIALS

330 yards (300m) of knitting worsted (yarn shown: Jarol Supersaver White DK)

Size F/5 (4.50mm) and size G/6 (3.50mm) hooks

Yarn scraps for nose and scarf; black for hat, eyes, mouth, and buttons

4-inch- (10cm-) dia circle of cardboard for base

5-inch- (12cm-) dia circle of white fabric to cover cardboard

1½-inch- (3.5cm-) dia circle of cardboard for hat

Washable stuffing

Tapestry and sewing needles

Pencil

GAUGE

1st 9 rounds = 4 inches (10cm) dia

HEIGHT

Approx 8 inches (20cm)

BODY

With larger hook, ch 4. Join with sl st into circle.

Round 1: 8sc into circle.

Round 2: 2sc into each st to end.

Round 3: *2sc into next st, 1sc into foll st. Rep from * to end.

Round 4: *1sc into each of next 3sts, 2sc into next st. Rep from * to end. (30sts.)

Round 5: *2sc into next st, 1sc into each of next 5sts. Rep from * to end.

Round 6: Sc to end.

Round 7: *1sc into each of next 4sts, 2sc into next st. Rep from * to end.

Rounds 8 and 9: Rep Rnds 5 and 6 once more.

Round 10: 1sc into each of next 4sts, *2sc into next st, 1sc into each of next 6sts.

Rep from * to last 3sts, 2sc into next st, 2sc. (56sts.)

Round 11: As Rnd 6.

Rounds 12–30: Continuing in sc, dec 1 st in varying positions over each of the next 18 rounds, and 2sts on the foll round (Rnd 30). After a few rounds, temporarily hold stitch on hook with safety pin and stitch fabric to RS base with a small hem enclosing the 4-inch (10cm) dia circle of cardboard.

Round 31: Ch 16 for first arm, 1sc into next st on body, work 17 more sc on body, ch 16 for other arm, 1sc into each of next 3sts on body, sc2tog, work 13sc to end.

Round 32: 1sc into each of 1st 16ch, 1sc into each of next 2sts, sc2tog, sc to next 16ch, 1sc into each ch st, sc to end. (66sts.)

Rounds 33–40: Incorporating arms, work 8 rounds of sc, dec 1 st in varying positions over each round on body front and back but not arms, 8 decs in all.

Round 41: Sc to end, dec 1 st on both body front and back. (56sts.)

Round 42: *Skip next 21sts, (2sc into next st, 1sc into each of next 2sts) twice, 2sc into next st. Rep from * once more. (20sts.)

Round 43: *1sc into next st, 2sc into next st. Rep from * to end. (30sts.)

Round 44: Sc to end.

Round 45: *1sc into each of next 4sts, 2sc into next st. Rep from * to end.

Rounds 46–51: Sc to end.

Round 52: *Skip next st, 1sc into each of next 5sts. Rep from * to end.

Rounds 53 and 54: Sc to end.

Round 55: *Skip next st, 1sc into each of next 4sts. Rep from * to end.

Round 56: *Skip next st, 1sc into each of next 3sts. Rep from * to end.

Round 57: *Skip next st, 1sc into each of next 2sts. Rep from * to end.

Round 58: *Skip next st, 1sc into foll st. Rep from * to end. Break yarn.

Darn in end, closing hole at top of head.

On RS, ladder-stitch underarms, tucking corners inside to make rounded ends. Beg with head, stuff completely, and then gather neck a little with some running stitches. Close above arms, again tucking corners inside.

◆

HAT

Rounds 1–3: Work as for Snowman to the end of Rnd 3.

Rounds 4–8: Sc to end.

Round 9: (2sc into next st, 1sc into each of next 7sts) 3 times.

Rounds 10 and 11: Sc to end.

Round 12: *1sc into next st, 2sc into next st. Rep from * to last st, 1sc.

Round 13: Sc to end.

Round 14: Sl st to end.

Break yarn.

◆

HAT LINING

Work as for Snowman to end of Rnd 3. Break yarn. Fit 1½-inch- (3.5cm-) dia circle of cardboard into hat and sew in lining to cover.

◆

NOSE

With smaller hook, ch 3. Join with sl st into circle.

Round 1: 6sc into circle.

Round 2: (1sc into each of next 2sts, 2sc into next st) twice.

Round 3: Sc to end, make 1sl st.

Sew nose onto face.

◆

SCARF

With larger hook, ch 47.

Work into single uppermost loops only on all rows.

Row 1: 1sc into 2nd ch from hook, 1sc into each foll ch to end, turn.

Rows 2–4: Ch 2 (1st sc), 1sc into each foll st to end. Break yarn.

To make two tiny white snowball bobbles for scarf ends, place approx 7 inches (18cm) yarn along the length of a pencil. Wind more yarn around the pencil and length of yarn, 30 or 40 turns, staying around the center of the pencil, and cut. Holding short yarn ends, slide yarn off pencil and tie very securely. Cut through loops and trim.

Gather scarf ends and attach bobbles. Embroider eyes, mouth, and 3 buttons down front to complete.

BASKET

A charming and unusual gift, this pretty basket could be lined with a circle of net or pretty fabric, and filled with homemade candy or with a dainty arrangement of dried, silk, or even fresh flowers in florist's foam.

MATERIALS

87 yards (80m) of size 5 crochet cotton (yarn shown: Coats Crochet Cotton No. 5)
Size 4 steel (1.75mm) hook
2 yards (2m) matching knitting worsted for cord handle
⅞ yard (80cm) of ¼-inch- (6mm-) wide ribbon
Fabric stiffener

GAUGE/MEASUREMENTS

Base = 3 inches (8cm) dia
Side = 1¼–1½ inches (3–4cm) tall
Top = 5½ inches (14cm) dia

BASE

Ch 5. Join with sl st into circle.

Round 1: Ch 3 (1st dc), 14dc into circle, sl st into top of 3ch.

Round 2: Ch 3 (1st dc), 1dc into same place as 3ch, 2dc into each foll st to end, sl st into top of 3ch. (30sts.)

Round 3: Ch 3 (1st dc), 1dc into same place as 3ch, 1dc into next st, *2dc into next st, 1dc into foll st. Rep from * to end, sl st into top of 3ch.

Round 4: Ch 3 (1st dc), 1dc into next st, 2dc into next st, *1dc into each of next 2sts, 2dc into next st. Rep from * to end, sl st into top of 3ch. (60sts.)

Round 5: Ch 3 (1st dc), 1dc into each of next 2sts, 2dc into next st, *1dc into each of next 3sts, 2dc into next st. Rep from * to end, sl st into top of 3ch.

Round 6: Ch 1 (1st sc), 1sc into each foll st to end, inc 5sc evenly over round. Sl st into 1st sc. (80 sts.)

SIDE

Round 7: Ch 2 (1st hdc), 1hdc into each foll st. to end, sl st into top of 2ch.

Round 8: (RS) Ch 6 (1st hdc + 4ch), skip next 3sts, *1hdc into next st, ch 4, skip next 3 sts. Rep from * to end, sl st into 2nd of 6ch. (20sps.)

Round 9: Ch 6 (1st hdc + 4ch), *1hdc into next hdc, working into st slightly left of top of stem, ch 4. Rep from * to end, sl st into 2nd of 6ch.

Rounds 10–13: Ch 7 (1st hdc + 5ch), *1hdc into next hdc, ch 5. Rep from * to end, sl st into 2nd of 7ch.

Round 14: Ch 8 (1st hdc + 6ch), *1hdc into next hdc, ch 6. Rep from * to end, sl st into 2nd of 8ch.

Round 15: Ch 9 (1st hdc + 7ch), *1hdc into next hdc, ch 7. Rep from * to end, sl st into 2nd of 9ch. Turn.

Round 16: (WS) Ch 5. Into same place as 5ch, work (1dc, ch 2) twice and (1dc, ch 1) once. Work 1sc into next 7ch sp, ch 1. *Into next hdc (top right), work (1dc, ch 2) 3 times and (1dc, ch 1) once, 1sc into next 7ch sp, ch 1. Rep from * to end, sl st into 3rd of 5ch. Break yarn and fasten off.

HANDLE

Either use one of the braids described on pages 121–2, or make a twisted cord using 4 strands of crochet cotton and 2 strands of knitting worsted—each 1 yard (1m) in length (see Techniques).

To complete the basket, apply fabric stiffener. During drying process, adjust slant of hdc sts as required and level outer edging of Rnd 16. Place over upturned jar to dry.

Thread handle through two 7ch sps on basket. Knot or loop and sew ends neatly in place. Coat handle with fabric stiffener, place jar or similar object inside basket to prop up handle, and shape handle during drying process.

Cut ribbon in half. Tie two small bows around handle base, above basket rim.

FLORAL CARD

❋❋

Create a nostalgic greeting card with this pretty embroidery on a padded background. The crochet edging is worked in the same shades of embroidery floss as the central flowers.

MATERIALS

Handkerchief lawn (or any suitable fabric)
6¼ × 8 inches (16 × 20cm)
Same color felt 4¾ × 6¼ inches (12 × 16cm)
6-strand embroidery floss for leaves, flowers, and edging
Crewel needle
2 pieces card stock 7 × 11 inches (18 × 28cm)
and 4¾ × 6¼ inches (12 × 16cm)
All-purpose glue
Felt scraps for flower centers
Size 8 steel (1.25mm) hook

MEASUREMENTS

5½ × 7 inches (14 × 18cm)

INSTRUCTIONS

1 With 2 strands of floss, smoothly and evenly embroider leaf design in the center of the fabric (see below). Press.
2 Fold larger card down center to measure 5½ inches (14cm) wide × 7 inches (18cm) long.
3 Apply ½-inch- (1cm-) wide strip of glue all around edge of smaller card, and affix felt, flattening out from center. Do not trim.
4 Trim embroidered fabric to approx ⅝ inch (1.5cm) larger all around than smaller card. (Keep embroidery centered.)

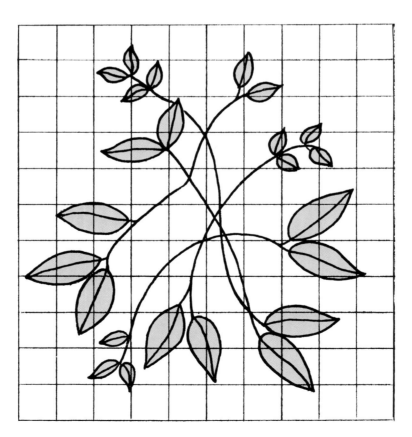

Guide for embroidering leaf and stem tracery on fabric.

Actual size

5 Place felt side of card onto back of embroidery. Keeping fabric fairly taut, turn edges under and glue to back of card, applying extra glue at corners as necessary.

6 Glue onto center of front of folded card.

7 With 2 strands of floss (or small amounts of fine crochet cotton), make 2 crocheted flowers following the pattern, and 2 or 3 more flowers with fewer petals.

BASIC FLOWER

Ch 7. Join with sl st into circle.

*Ch 8, 1dc into 4th ch from hook, 1dc into each of next 3ch, 1hdc into next ch, 1sc into circle.

Rep from * until 11 petals. Fasten off.

Arrange flowers on embroidered leaves. Glue backs around center hole and glue down. Add small circles of felt for flower centers.

EDGING

Ch 285 using 2 strands of embroidery floss.

Check ch for (ample) fit around folded fabric edge and adjust sts as necessary.

Row 1: 1hdc into 3rd ch from hook, 1hdc into each foll ch to end, turn.

Row 2: Ch 3 (1st dc), 1dc into next st, ch 3, 1hdc around stem of last dc made, skip next st, *1dc into each of next 2sts, ch 3, 1hdc around stem of last dc made, skip next st.

Rep from * until end of ch is reached.

Break yarn and fasten off.

Glue base ch and 1st row to fabric edge so that ruffle sits neatly on card edge, making a tiny pinch for corners. Glue ruffle at corners. Cut edging to correct length and neatly glue down end.

HIGH-WHEELER CARD

❊ ❊

A really Victorian effect is produced with this charming card. Work the edging in the same way as for the Floral Card.

MATERIALS

Handkerchief lawn (or any suitable fabric)
6¼ × 8 inches (16 × 20cm)
Same color felt 4¾ × 6¼ inches (12 × 16cm)
6-strand embroidery floss for letters,
bicycle, road, and edging
Crewel needle
2 pieces card stock 7 × 11 inches (18 × 28cm)
and 4¾ × 6¼ inches (12 × 16cm)
Fabric marker
All-purpose glue
Size 8 steel (1.25mm) hook

MEASUREMENTS

5½ × 7 inches (14 × 18cm)

INSTRUCTIONS

1 With 2 strands of floss, embroider design, but only mark wheel positions (see p. 115). Follow Steps 2–6 as for floral card.

7 Crochet a large and small wheel, following instructions.

Press.

LARGE WHEEL

Ch 5 using 2 strands of embroidery floss. Join with sl st into circle.

Round 1: Ch 1, 10sc into circle, sl st into 1st sc.

Round 2: (ch 24, 1sc into next sc) 9 times, ch 24, 1sc into base of 1st 24ch.

Break yarn and fasten off.

Round 3: With RS facing, rejoin to top of any 24ch sp, ch 1 (1st sc), 4sc into same sp, ch 4, *5sc into next sp, ch 4.

Rep from * to end, sl st into 1st sc.

Round 4: Into each sp (over 5sc or 4ch), work 5sc. End with sl st into 1st sc.

Round 5: Ch 1 (1st sc), 1sc into each of next 3sc, skip next sc, *1sc into each of next 4sc, skip next sc.

Rep from * to end, sl st into 1st sc.

SMALL WHEEL

Ch 4 using 1 strand of embroidery floss. Join with sl st into circle.

Celebration

Round 1: (ch 10, 1sc into circle) 6 times. Break yarn and fasten off.

Round 2: With RS facing, rejoin to any 10ch sp, ch 1 (1st sc), 2sc into same sp, ch 3, *3sc into next sp, ch 3.

Rep from * to end, sl st into 1st sc.

Round 3: Into each sp (over 3sc or 3ch), work 3sc. End with sl st into 1st sc.

Round 4: Ch 1 (1st sc), 1sc into each foll st to end, sl st into 1st sc.

Glue centers and rims of wheels, and fix in place. Make edging and complete as for floral card.

◆

<u>VARIATIONS</u>

1 In place of embroidery, paint on the background using a fabric marker.

2 Using the oval on top of a tissue box as a template, draw an oval in center of fabric. Cover drawn line with an edging, and fill oval with miniature crocheted flowers. Complete with a small bow.

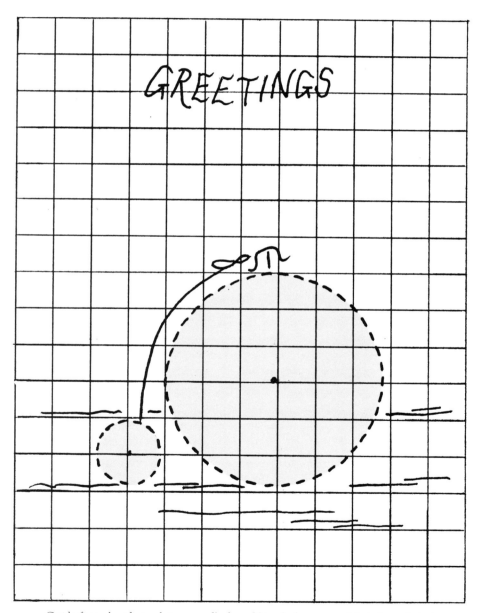

Guide for embroidering letters, roadbed, and bicycle frame onto fabric (actual size).
Mark wheel positions, but do not embroider

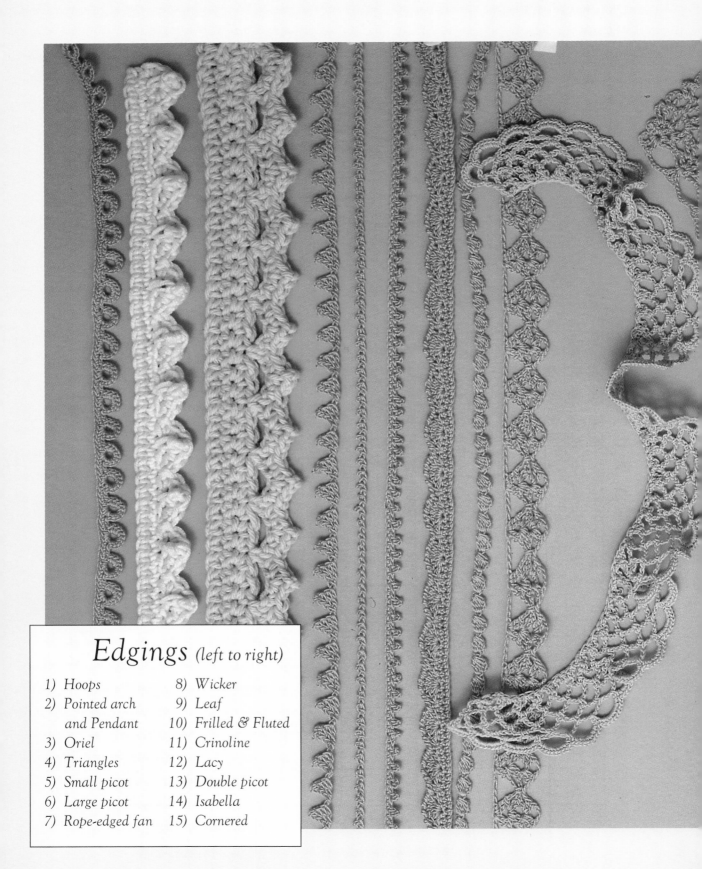

Edgings (left to right)

1) Hoops
2) Pointed arch and Pendant
3) Oriel
4) Triangles
5) Small picot
6) Large picot
7) Rope-edged fan
8) Wicker
9) Leaf
10) Frilled & Fluted
11) Crinoline
12) Lacy
13) Double picot
14) Isabella
15) Cornered

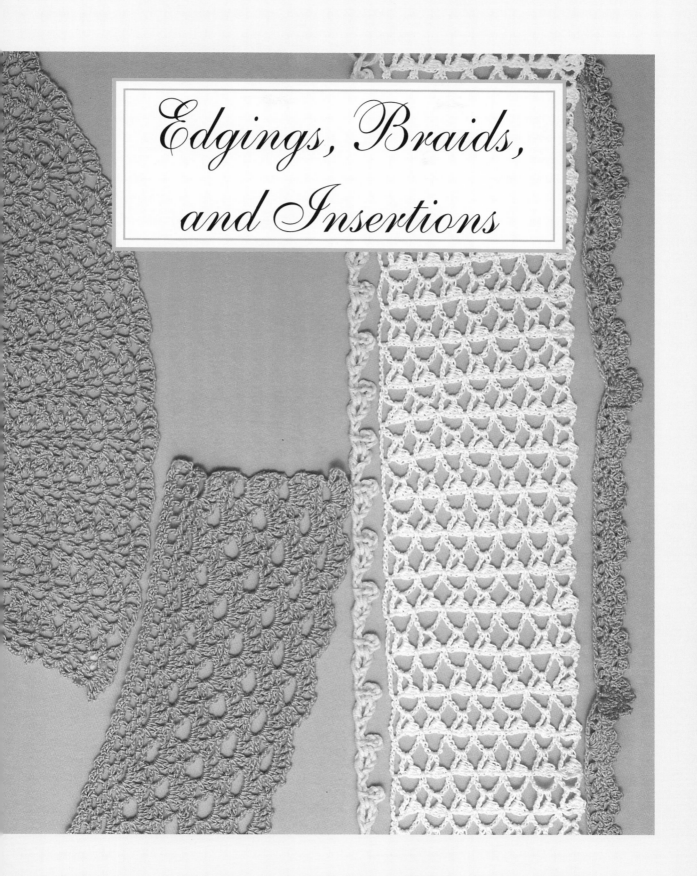

Edgings, Braids, and Insertions

Adding a trimming enhances household items, gifts, or clothes, both old and new. An old armchair, for example, gets a new lease on life when an elegant braid is added around its base. Bedroom curtains and lamp shades can be tied in with the color scheme of the room with specially made trimmings. There are so many effects you can achieve, simply and quickly, with the thoughtful use of edgings and braids. Insertions can be used either to lengthen or simply to decorate. For example, a plain blouse can be transformed into something charming and original with a crochet insertion, either by cutting the fabric and attaching the insertion to both cut edges, or simply by placing the crochet over the fabric and stitching it in position.

Braids and insertions can be used in another way, too. Strips can be sewn edge to edge to create attractive fabrics to be used in their own right—for example, for covering pillows or chair cushions. The possibilities are endless, so try some of the effects explained in this chapter, then apply them whenever you like. They may transform your crochet—and your home.

EDGINGS

♦

HOOPS

Ch 6. Work 1sc into 6th ch from hook, *ch 9, 1sc into 6th ch from hook.
Rep from * to required length.
Work back along straight edge with loops below as follows:
Row 1: 2sc into 1st loop, *1sc into each of next 3ch between loops, 2sc into next loop.
Rep from * to end.
Row 2: With loops above, cont by working another 9sc into 1st loop, *1sl st into each of next 3 single base ch opp 3sc grp of last row, 9sc into next loop.
Rep from * to end, sl st into 1st st of last row.

♦

POINTED ARCH
AND PENDANT

Make a ch divisible by 4 plus 1 to required length.
Row 1: 1sc into 2nd ch from hook, sc to end, turn.
Row 2: (RS) Ch 1 (1st st), 1sc into each foll sc but instead of working in the usual way, insert hook under and work into each single horizontal st (facing) below top ch of scs. (Sts = even no.) Turn.
Row 3: Ch 3, skip 1st and next st, 1sl

st into each of next 3sts, *ch 3, skip next st, 1sl st into each of next 3sts. Rep from * ending with 2sl sts, turn.
Row 4: Ch 1 (1st st), skip next sl st. *Into next 3ch loop, work 2sc, 1tr (over and in front of loop) into skipped st of Row 3. Ease same loop toward left of tr stem, work 2sc into this loop, 1sl st (over sl st) into same sc as 2nd of 3sl st of Row 3, pull stem and top of tr forward. Rep from * but end row with 1sc into edge st.

♦

ORIEL

Make a ch divisible by 3 plus 2 to required length.
Row 1: 1sc into 2nd ch from hook, sc to end, turn.
Rows 2 and 3: Ch 1 (1st st), sc to end, turn.
Row 4: Ch 5, skip 1st and next 2 sts, 1sl st into next st, *ch 5, skip next 2sts, 1sl st into next st.
Rep from * to end, turn.
Row 5: Ch 2, skip 1st ch st of loop, *1sc into each of next 2 ch sts, ch 2, 1sc into same st as last sc made, 1sc into 4th ch st, (skip 5th ch st, sl st, and 1st ch st of next loop).
Rep from * working final loop as before but end with 1sc into edge st.

TRIANGLES

*Ch 5, 1sc into 2nd ch from hook, 1hdc into 3rd, 1dc into 4th, 1tr into 5th ch from hook.
Rep from * to required length.

♦

SMALL PICOT

*Ch 3, 1sc into 3rd ch from hook.
Rep from * to required length.

♦

LARGE PICOT

(See below.)
Make an odd number of ch sts to required length.

A simple picot. Ch 3. Inserting hook through top and side of last sc made, make 1sl st.

Work 1sc into 2nd ch from hook, *ch 3, insert hook through top loop and left vertical loop of last sc made and make 1sl st, 1sc into each of next 2ch.

Rep from * ending with 1sc instead of 2sc.

ROPE-EDGED FAN

Make a ch divisible by 6 plus 2 to required length.

Row 1: 1sc into 2nd ch from hook, sc to end, turn.

Row 2: Ch 1 (1st st), sc to end, turn.

Row 3: (RS) Ch 1 (1st st), *skip next 2sts, 6dc into next st, skip next 2sts, 1sl st into same sc (in Row 1) as next st (skip sc above).

Rep from * to end, working last sl st into final st of Row 2. Do not turn.

Row 4: Ch 1. Work reverse sc back along dcs of Row 3, skipping each sl st as follows:

With RS still facing, twist this end of work so as to insert hook (from front) downward into (normal position) last dc made, yo, draw yarn through, and complete 1sc as usual. Rep into each dc until end, 1sl st into 1st st of last row.

WICKER

Ch 4.

4dc bobble into 4th ch from hook (= 4dc into one st, omitting the 3rd stage of each dc, so that the loops increase on the hook, i.e. yo, insert hook into st, yo, draw loop through, yo, draw loop through 2 of the loops on hook and omit the foll 3rd stage of the dc. Rep into the same st [4th ch], leaving 3 loops on hook, rep into the same st, leaving 4 loops on hook, rep into the same st, yo, draw yarn through all 5 loops on hook), *ch 5, 4dc bobble into 4th ch from hook.

Rep from * to required length. (Back of work is RS.)

LEAF

Make a ch divisible by 6 minus 2 to required length.

Row 1: (1dc, ch 2, 2dc) into 4th ch from hook, *ch 5, skip next 5 base ch, (2dc, ch 2, 2dc) into next ch.

Rep from * to end, turn.

Row 2: Ch 3 (1dc, ch 2, 2dc) into 1st 2ch sp, *ch 3, (2dc, ch 2, 2dc) into next 2ch sp.

Rep from * to end, turn.

Row 3: Ch 3 (1dc, ch 3, 2dc) into 1st 2ch sp, *ch 1, 1sc under 5ch and 3ch of prev 2 rows, ch 1 (2dc, ch 3, 2dc) into next 2ch sp.

Rep from * to end, sl st into end dc.

FRILLED AND FLUTED

Make a fairly tight ch divisible by 4 minus 2 to required length.

Row 1: 1sc into 6th ch from hook, *ch 5, skip next 3 base ch, 1sc into next ch.

Rep from * to end, turn.

Row 2: Ch 5, 1sc into 1st 5ch sp, *ch 5, 1sc into next 5ch sp.

Rep from * to end (including last sp), turn.

Rep last row 12 times more, or as required.

Final row: (RS) 10sc into each 5ch sp. Break yarn and fasten off.

For gathered heading: with RS facing, work along base ch edge, join yarn, ch 1, and make 1sc into each 3ch sp with 1sc into each sc stem.

If desired, a length of narrow ribbon can be threaded through top row of spaces.

CRINOLINE

Ch 5, 1sl st into 5th ch from hook, *ch 12, 1sl st into 5th ch from hook.

Rep from * to required length.

Row 1: Ch 4. Working along sl st side of base ch: into 1st loop, over sl st, work (1dc, ch 1, 1dc), ch 6, *(keep base ch untwisted) 1dc into next loop, (ch 1, 1dc) twice into same loop, ch 6.

Rep from * to last loop, (1dc, ch 1) twice into loop, ch 3, 1sl st into same loop.

Row 2: Working back along opp side of loops:

ch 4, (1dc, ch 1) 4 times into 1st loop, *1sc around center of next 7ch, ch 1, (1dc, ch 1) 4 times into next loop.

Rep from * to end.

Work 1 extra dc into last loop, turn.

Row 3: Sl st to and into 2nd sp between dcs, ch 5, 1dc into same sp, (ch 2, 1dc) twice into each of next 2sps, *(skip next 2 sps). Over next center 3sps, (1dc, ch 2, 1dc) into 1st sp, (ch 2, 1dc) twice into each of foll 2 sps.

Rep from * to end disregarding final sp, turn.

Rep last row to required depth.

LACY

Make a ch divisible by 8 plus 4 to required length.

Row 1: 1dc into 6th ch from hook, *ch 1, skip next ch, 1dc into next ch.

Rep from * to end.

Row 2: Working along base ch side, ch 4, 1sc into 1st sp, *ch 3, 1sc into next sp. Rep from * to end.

Row 3: Working along straight edge, rep last row, working (again) into 1st sp but not last loop, turn.

Cont on same side.

Row 4: 2sc into 1st 3ch sp, *ch 5, skip next 3ch, 1sc into next 3ch sp.

Rep from * to end, turn.

Row 5: 1sc into 1st 5ch sp, ch 5. Into same sp, work (2dc, ch 2) twice and 1dc, *ch 2, 1sc into next 5ch sp, ch 2. Into next sp, work a scallop— (1dc, ch 2, 1dc) 3 times.

Rep from * to end, turn.

Row 6: 1sc into 1st sp, ch 6, skip next (center) sp of scallop, 1sc into next sp, *ch 5, skip next 2 sps in between, 1sc into 1st sp of next scallop, ch 6, 1sc into 3rd sp of same scallop.

Rep from * to end, turn.

Row 7: 1sc into 1st sp, ch 5, 1sc into both 1st (6ch sp and center 2ch sp of prev row) tog, ch 2, *(1dc, ch 2, 1dc) 3 times into next 5ch sp, ch 2, 1sc into both next (6ch sp and center 2ch sp of prev row) tog, ch 2.

Rep from * to end, 1dc into end sc, turn.

Row 8: 1sc into 1st sp, ch 5, *1sc into 1st sp of next 3-sp scallop, ch 6, skip center sp of scallop, 1sc into next sp, ch 5, skip 2 sps in between.

Braids

1) Epaulet
2) Elizabeth
3) Sailor's scroll
4) Slip-stitch cord
5) Two-piece
6) Wheels
7) Firestone
8) Cannich loops
9) Abigail
10) Two colors

Rep from * to end, 1sc into end sc, turn.

Row 9: 1sc into 1st sp, ch 5. Into same sp, work (2dc, ch 2) twice and 1dc, *ch 2, 1sc into both next (6ch sp and center 2ch sp of prev row) tog, ch 2, (1dc, ch 2, 1dc) 3 times into next 5ch sp.

Rep from * to end, turn.

Rep Rows 6–9 to required depth.

DOUBLE PICOT

*Ch 4, 1dc into 3rd ch from hook, ch 4, 1sc into last loop made.

Rep from * to required length.

ISABELLA

Ch 41 (or any no. divisible by 5 plus 1 to required depth).

Row 1: 1sc into 11th ch from hook, *ch 7, skip next 4 base ch, 1sc into next ch.

Rep from * to end, turn.

Row 2: (RS) Ch 7, 2tr into 1st loop.

(Insert hook from front into sp between last 2tr made), work (sc, 1hdc, 1dc) around last tr stem, *2tr into next loop, (1sc, 1hdc, 1dc) around last tr stem.

Rep from * to last loop, (1tr, 1dtr) into loop, (1sc, 1hdc, 1dc) around dtr stem.

Ease trs to loop centers of prev row. Turn.

Row 3: Skip dtr, 1tr into 1st tr, ch 6, 1sc into sp (diamond-shaped) between 1st tr and foll dc, *ch 7, skip next tr pair, 1sc into same-shaped sp, just before foll dc.

Rep from * to last loop, ch 7, 1sc into 7ch sp (over 7th of 7ch), turn.

Rep last 2 rows to required length. This edging can be left as it is, or gathered along looped edge.

CORNERED

Ch 4, *sc into 4th ch from hook (corner loop made), ch 9, (1dc into 4th ch from hook, ch 9) required no. of times to position for next corner loop.

Rep from * to fit rem sides, omitting 4ch sts at end, sl st (untwisted) into 1st st.

Row 1: 1sl st into 1st loop, ch 3 (dc), 8dc into same loop, (1dc, ch 2, 1dc) into 3rd of next 5ch, *7dc into next loop, easing sts tog toward loop center, (1dc, ch 2, 1dc) into 3rd of next 5ch.

Rep from * to end, but working 9dc into each corner loop.

Row 2: Into each of 1st, 3rd, 5th, 7th, and 9th dc of next 9dc group, work (1sl st, ch 4, 1dc into 4th ch from hook = rose), skip next (1dc, 2ch, 1dc).

*Into each of 1st, 3rd, 5th, and 7th dc of next 7dc group, work a rose, skip next (1dc, ch 2, 1dc).

Rep from * to end, but working an extra rose at each corner. Sl st into 1st st.

BRAIDS

♦

EPAULET

Make a ch divisible by 3 minus 1 to required length.

Row 1: 1sc into 2nd ch from hook, sc to end, turn.

Row 2: (RS) Ch 2 (1st st), 1hdc into next st, *(loosen loop on hook). Around stem of last hdc made, work 1st stage of 1dc as follows: Yo, insert hook (from the front) under stem, yo, bring hooked loop forward (3 loops on hook). Work 2 more 1st stages around same stem, yo, draw through all 7 loops on hook. Skip next free sc, 1hdc into each of next 2sts.

Rep from * ending row with only 1hdc, turn.

Row 3: Ch 2 (1st st), sc evenly to end.

ELIZABETH

Make 6ch.

Row 1: Work 2dc into 3rd ch from hook, skip 2ch, 1sc into end ch, turn.

Row 2: Ch 3, 2dc into 3rd ch from hook, skip next 2dc worked in last row, 1sc into top of end 2ch, turn.

Rep Row 2 to required length.

SAILOR'S SCROLL

Make ch to required length.

Keeping final loop of each st fairly tight, work 1tr into 5th ch from hook, tr to end. Do not turn. Work 4sc around end tr stem. Twisting and turning work as necessary, with same side still facing, work 1sc around and enclosing base ch between last 2tr made.

Turn work clockwise and work 4sc around next (2nd) tr stem.

Turn to reverse side and work 1sc (enclosing top of trs) between 2nd and 3rd tr.

Turn to front again, 4sc around next (3rd) tr stem, 1sc around base ch between 3rd and 4th trs.

Cont to end, working the 4sc from the front around every tr, and 1sc alternately along sides (1sc between every two tr along an edge.)

SLIP-STITCH CORD

Make ch to required length.

Work 1sl st into 2nd and each foll single horizontal st behind each ch.

TWO-PIECE

(Use yarn in two colors of equal thickness.) With 1st color, *ch 3, 1sc into 3rd ch from hook.

Rep from * to required length. Break off 1st color.

Do not turn—work Row 1 back along straighter edge.

Row 1: (RS) Join 2nd color with ch 2, 1sc into st above 1st picot, work a 2nd sc into part of ch st showing between 1st 2 picots, 1sc into st above 2nd picot.

Cont similarly to end (with 1sc between picots and 1sc above each picot). Work 1sc after final picot.

Make another piece exactly the same. Line up opposite picots and sew the 2 pieces together on WS along straight edges.

WHEELS

Ch 5. Join with sl st into circle.

Row 1: Ch 2, work 9hdc into circle, sl st into top of 2ch.

Row 2: Ch 7, (1tr into next hdc, ch 3) 9 times, sl st into 4th of 7ch.

Row 3: Ch 1, 1sc into same place as 1ch, 3sc into next sp, *2sc into next tr, 3sc into next sp.

Rep from * to end, sl st into 1ch.

Row 4: 1sl st into each foll st to end. Ch 14. Work 1sl st into 5th ch from hook, to make a circle. Keeping the 9 linking ch behind work, rep from Row 1 to required length.

FIRESTONE

Make ch to required length.
(RS facing) Picking up top strand only for all sts, work 1sc into 2nd ch from hook, sc to end. Break yarn and fasten off. Rejoining at slip-knot, ch 2 for 1st st, sc back along opp side of ch, picking up single strands as before. Break yarn, fasten off, and sew in ends.

The braid can be used as it is, or decorated in a variety of ways. Some suggestions:

1 Weave narrow ribbon through central eyelets.

2 Crochet a chain along center; or make a separate chain and sew down with another color.

CANNICH LOOPS

*Ch 3, 1dc into 3rd ch from hook. Rep from * to required length.

Round 1: Ch 3, 1sc around dc stem into 1st loop, *ch 3, 1sc into next loop. Rep from * to end.

Work around end with (ch 3, 1sc into same loop) twice.

Cont back along unworked side with the same patt, (ch 3, 1sc into next loop) to end.

Work another 3ch, 1sc into same end loop, sl st into 1st loop of round.

ABIGAIL

Ch 5.

Row 1: 1hdc into 3rd ch from hook, 1hdc into each of next 2ch, turn.

Row 2: Ch 2 (1st hdc), 1hdc between 1st 2hdc, 1hdc between 2nd and 3rd hdc, 1hdc between 3rd and 4th hdc, turn.

Rep last row until required length. Do not turn after final row.

Over stem of end hdc of each row, work along edge: 1sl st over 1st hdc stem, *2sc over next hdc stem, 1sl st over next hdc stem.

Rep from * to end of braid.

With same side facing, similarly complete 2nd edge, with 2sc opp 2sc, 1sl st opp 1sl st.

TWO COLORS

With col A, make no. of ch divisible by 4 to required length.

Row 1: (RS) 1dc into 4th ch from hook, *ch 2, skip next 2ch, 1dc into each of next 2ch.

Rep from * to end. Break yarn and fasten off.

Row 2: (RS facing) Join col B between 1st 2dc. Work along edge: ch 1, *5sc into next 2ch sp, 1sl st between next 2dc.

Rep from * to end. Break yarn and fasten off. Work similarly along 2nd edge.

Row 3: (RS facing) Join col A between 1st 2dc of Row 1, ch 3 (dc), dc3tog (including 1st dc) in same place. *Over next 5sc, skip 1st sc, 1sc into each of next 3sc, skip next sc, dc3tog inserting hook between next 2dc of Row 1.

Rep from * to end.

Work similarly along 2nd edge.

INSERTIONS

FILET

Ch 18.

Row 1: 1dc into 4th ch from hook, 1dc into each of next 5ch, ch 2, skip next 2ch, 1dc into each of next 7ch, turn.

Row 2: (First 3ch counts as 1st dc in this and foll rows.) Ch 3, 1dc into each of next 3sts, ch 2, skip next 2 sts, 1dc into next st, 2dc into next 2ch sp, 1dc into next st, ch 2, skip next 2 sts, 1dc into each of next 4sts, turn.

Row 3: Ch 3, 1dc into each of next 3sts, ch 2, skip next 2ch, 1dc into next st, ch 2, skip next 2sts, 1dc into next st, ch 2, skip next 2ch, 1dc into each of next 4sts, turn.

Row 4: Ch 3, 1dc into each of next 3sts, ch 2, skip next 2ch, 1dc into next st, 2dc into next 2ch sp, 1dc into next st, ch 2, skip next 2ch, 1dc into each of next 4sts, turn.

Row 5: Ch 3, 1dc into each of next 3sts, 2dc into next 2ch sp, 1dc into next st, ch 2, skip next 2sts, 1dc into next st, 2dc into next 2ch sp, 1dc into each of next 4sts, turn.

Rep Rows 2–5 until required length is reached.

◆

LONG CHECKERS

Ch 18.

Row 1: 1tr into 5th ch from hook, 1tr into next ch, (ch 3, skip next 3ch, 1tr into each of next 3ch) twice, turn.

Row 2: Ch 6, skip 1st 3tr block, 1tr into each of next 3ch, ch 3, skip next 3tr, 1tr into each of next 3ch, ch 2, skip next 2tr, 1tr into end st, turn.

Row 3: Ch 4 (tr), 1tr into each of next 2ch, (ch 3, skip next 3tr, 1tr into each of next 3ch) twice, turn.

Rep last 2 rows to required length.

◆

BUTTONS

*Ch 3, 1dc into 3rd ch from hook. Rep from * to required length with even no. of dcs.

Round 1: Ch 3, 1sc around dc stem into 1st loop, *ch 3, 1sc into next loop.

Rep from * to end. Work (ch 3, 1sc into same end loop) twice more. Mark last loop made.

Rep from * along unworked side to end, working only 1 extra loop into end loop, instead of 2. This is last loop of 2nd side. Do not turn.

Round 2: 2sc into 1st 3ch loop of Rnd 1. Work (7dc into next loop, 1sc into foll loop) to marked loop. Make another sc into last loop, ch 2 2sc into marked loop.

Work (7dc into next loop, 1sc into foll loop) to end of 2nd side, making another sc into last loop. Ch 2, 1sl st into 1st sc of round.

Round 3: Ch 7 (1sc, ch 2, 1sc) into 4th of next 7dc, *ch 6, (1sc, ch 2, 1sc) into 4th of next 7dc.

Rep from * to end of 1st side, ch 7, 3sc into 2ch sp, ch 7, (1sc, ch 2, 1sc) into 4th of next 7dc.

Rep from * to end of 2nd side, ch 7, 3sc into 2ch sp.

Round 4: Ch 7, 1hdc into 6th ch st of next 7ch, ch 2, 1hdc into next ch st, ch 2, *1hdc into 1st ch st of next 6ch, ch 2, 1hdc into next ch st, ch 2, 1hdc into 5th ch st of same 6ch, ch 2, 1hdc into next ch st, ch 2.

Rep from * to end of 6ch loops, 1st side.

Work 1hdc into 1st ch st of next 7ch, ch 2, 1hdc into next ch st, ch 7, 1sc into each of next 3sc, ch 7. Starting with 6th of next 7ch, cont same patt of hdcs and chs to end. Work into 1st and 2nd ch sts of last 7ch, ch 7, 1sc into each of next 2sc, 1sl st into next sc.

◆

SPIDER FLOWER

Ch 28.

Row 1: 1dc into 7th ch from hook, 1dc into each of next 18ch, ch 2, skip 2ch, 1dc into last ch, turn.

Row 2: Ch 5, skip 1st dc and next 2ch, 1dc into each of next 7dc, ch 4, skip next 2dc, 1tr into next dc, ch 4, skip next 2dc, 1dc into each of next 7dc, ch 2, skip 2ch, 1dc into next ch, turn.

Row 3: Ch 5, skip 1st dc and next ch 2, 1dc into each of next 5dc, ch 4, 1sc into 4th of next 4ch, 1sc into tr, 1sc into 1st of next 4ch, ch 4, skip next 2dc, 1dc into each of next 5dc, ch 2, skip 2ch, 1dc into next ch, turn.

Row 4: Ch 5, skip 1st dc and next 2ch, 1dc into each of next 3dc, ch 6, 1sc into each of 3sc, ch 6, skip next 2dc, 1dc into each of next 3dc, ch 2, skip 2ch, 1dc into next ch, turn.

Row 5: Ch 5, skip 1st dc and next 2ch, 1dc into each of next 3dc, 2dc into 6ch sp, ch 5, 1sc into each of 3sc, ch 5, 2dc into next 6ch sp, 1dc into each of next 3dc, ch 2, skip 2ch, 1dc into next ch, turn.

Row 6: Ch 5, skip 1st dc and next 2ch, 1dc into each of next 5dc, 2dc into 5ch sp, ch 2, 1tr into center sc, ch 2, 2dc into next 5ch sp, 1dc into each of next 5dc, ch 2, skip 2ch, 1dc into next ch, turn.

Row 7: Ch 5, skip 1st dc and next 2ch, 1dc into each of next 7dc, 2dc into next 2ch sp, 1dc into tr, 2dc into next 2ch sp, 1dc into each of next 7dc, ch 2, skip 2ch, 1dc into next ch, turn.

Rep Rows 2–7 to required length.

◆

JACOB'S LADDER

Ch 12.

Row 1: 1dc into 4th ch from hook, 1dc into next ch, ch 4, skip 4ch, 1dc into each of next 3ch, turn.

Row 2: Ch 3 (dc), 1dc into each of next 2dc, ch 4, skip 4ch, 1dc into each of next 3dc, turn.

Rep last row to required length.

◆

DAISY RINGS

Ch 4, 1tr into 4th ch from hook, *ch 6, 1tr into 4th ch from hook.

Rep from * to required length. Do not turn.

Round 1: (1st side) Around tr, into 1st loop, work petals as follows: 1sc and (ch 3, 1sc) 5 times into same loop, *ch 1 to next loop, 1sc and (ch 3, 1sc) 5 times into loop.

Rep from * to end.

Ch 3. Do not turn.

(2nd side) Into same end loop, work 1sc and (ch 3, 1sc) 5 times. With petals opposite petals, rep the 1ch and petals patt to end.

Ch 3, 1sl st into 1st sc. Do not turn.

Round 2: (1st side) ch 9, 1dc into space of 3rd of 1st 5 petals, *ch 5, 1dc into space of 3rd of next 5 petals.

Rep from * to end, ch 9, skip 4th and 5th petals, 1sl st into next petal. Work 2nd side to match 1st side.

Insertions

1) Filet
2) Long Checkers
3) Buttons
4) Spider Flower
5) Jacob's Ladder
6) Daisy Rings
7) Wheat Sheaf
8) Six-Petal Flower
9) Diamond Zigzag
10) Picot Motif

WHEAT SHEAF

Ch 12.

Row 1: 1dc into 4th ch from hook, ch 7, skip 6 base ch, 1dc into each of next 2ch, turn.

Row 2: Ch 3 (1st dc), 1dc into next dc, ch 6, skip 7ch, 1dc into each of next 2dc, turn.

Row 3: Ch 3 (1st dc), 1dc into next dc, ch 3, 1sc into sp to enclose 6ch and 7ch of prev 2 rows, ch 3, 1dc into each of next 2dc, turn.

Row 4: Ch 3 (1st dc), 1dc into next dc, ch 7, 1dc into each of next 2dc, turn.

Rep Rows 2–4 to required length, working final row of insertion as Row 4 but with ch 6 instead of ch 7. Do not turn after final row.

Work 1st side as follows: ch 1, insert hook into sp between last 2dc of final row, and work 2sc to enclose outer dc stem, *ch 8, skip next 2sps along edge, 2sc into next sp. Rep from * to end. Ch 11.

Complete 2nd side to match 1st side, ending with ch 10 and 1sl st into 1st st.

SIX-PETAL FLOWER

This insertion can be made of one or more strips of flowers, sewn together, to any depth required.

Ch 12. Join with sl st into circle.

Round 1: Ch 1, 24sc into circle, sl st into 1st sc.

Round 2: Ch 9, (skip next sc, 1sl st into each of next 3sc, ch 9) 5 times, skip next sc, 1sl st into each of next 2sc.

Round 3: *1sl st into 1st st of next 9ch, 1sc into each of next 3ch sts, 3sc into next st at center of ch loop, 1sc into each of next 3ch sts, 1sl st into next st. Rep from * to end, sl st into 1st st of round. Leave 8-inch (20cm) end. Break yarn and fasten off. Make the no. of flowers required, and join together.

To make a ch edging: with RS facing, join yarn to 1st petal tip, *ch 7, 1tr into sp between next 2 petals, ch 7, 1sc into next petal tip. Rep from * to end.

Work similarly along rem edge.

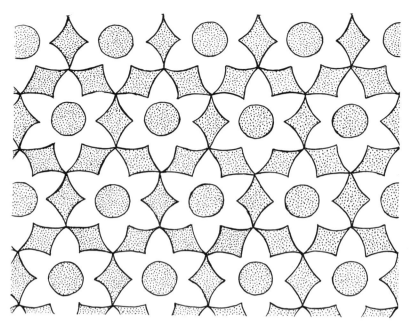

The pattern produced when six-petal flower motifs are sewn together

DIAMOND ZIGZAG

Ch 22, fairly loosely.

Row 1: 1sc into 6th ch from hook, *ch 3, skip next base ch, 1sc into next ch.

Rep from * to end, turn.

Row 2: Ch 3, 1sc into 1st loop, ch 3, 1sc into next loop, *3dc into next sc, 1sc into next loop, (ch 3, 1sc) into each of next 2 loops.

Rep from * once more, ch 3, 1sc into last loop, turn.

Row 3: Ch 3, 1sc into 1st loop, *(ch 3, 1sc) into each of next 2 loops, 3dc into next sc, 1sc into 2nd of next 3dc.

Rep from * once more, (ch 3, 1sc) into each of next 2 loops, turn.

Row 4: Ch 3, 1sc into 1st loop, ch 3, 1sc into next loop, ch 3, *1sc into 2nd of next 3dc, 3dc into next sc, (1sc, ch 3) into each of next 2 loops.

Rep from * once more, 1sc into last loop, turn.

Row 5: Ch 3, 1sc into 1st loop, ch 3, 1sc into next loop, *3dc into next sc, 1sc into 2nd of next 3dc, (ch 3, 1sc) into each of next 2 loops.

Rep from * once more, ch 3, 1sc into last loop, turn.

Rep Rows 3–5 to required length.

PICOT MOTIF

(Sewn directly onto fabric. Work 2 or 3 rounds.)

Ch 5. Join with sl st into circle.

Round 1: Ch 3 (1st dc), (ch 4, 1sc into 3rd ch from hook = picot, ch 1, 1dc into circle) 5 times, picot, ch 1, sl st into 1st dc. (6 picots.)

Note the single ch st at each side of picots.

Round 2: Sl st into ch st before 1st picot, ch 3 (1st dc), (picot, ch 1, 1dc into next ch st of prev round) 11 times to end.

Work 1 picot, ch 1, sl st into 1st dc. (12 picots.)

Round 3: Ch 3 (1st dc), picot, ch 1, skip 1st ch st of prev round, 1dc into ch st between 1st picot and foll dc, picot, ch 1, 1dc into ch st between same dc and foll picot, picot, ch 1, (1dc into next dc, picot, ch 1, skip next ch st of prev round, 1dc into ch st between next picot and foll dc, picot, ch 1, 1dc into ch st between same dc and foll picot, picot, ch 1) 5 times, sl st into 1st dc. (18 picots.)

Yarn Manufacturers/ Suppliers

UNITED STATES

Coats & Clarks, Inc.
30 Patewood Drive, Suite 351
Green, SC 29615
Tel: 803 234 0331

The DMC Corporation
Port Kearny, Building 10
South Kearny, NJ 07032
Tel: 201 589 0606

Knitting Fever, Inc.
180 Babylon Turnpike, Roosevelt, NY 11575
Tel: 516 546 3600

Plymouth Yarn Co., Inc.
500 Lafayette Street, Bristol, PA 19007
Tel: 215 788 0459

Rainbow Gallery, Inc.
7412 Fulton Avenue
North Hollywood, CA 91605
Tel: 818 982 4496

GREAT BRITAIN

Coats Patons Crafts
PO Box, McMullen Road
Darlington, Co Durham DL1 1YQ
Tel: 01325 381010

DMC Creative World Ltd.
Pullman Road
Wigston, Leicester LE18 2DY
Tel: 01533 811040

Jaeger Handknitting Ltd.
McMullen Road
Darlington, Co Durham DL1 1YQ
Tel: 01325 380123

Jarol Ltd.
White Rose Mills, Cape Street, Canal Road,
Bradford BD1 4RN
Tel: 01274 392274

Sirdar Ltd.
Flanshaw Lane, Alverthorpe, Wakefield,
West Yorkshire WF2 9ND
Tel: 01924 371501

Twilleys of Stamford Ltd.
Roman Mill, Stamford, Lincs PE9 1BG
Tel: 01780 52661

AUSTRALIA

Coats Patons Handknittings
89–91 Peters Avenue, Mulgrave, Victoria 3170
Tel: 03 5612288

DMC Needlecraft Pty Ltd.
51–66 Carrington Road, Marrickville, NSW 2204
Tel: 02 5593088

Panda Yarns Pty
314–320 Albert Street, Brunswick
Victoria 3056
Tel: 03 3803888

NEW ZEALAND

Coats Enzed Crafts
PO Box 58447
Green Mount
Auckland

Warnaar Trading Co., Ltd.
(DMC Threads)
PO Box 19–567
Christchurch

Index

Abbreviations, 2
Angel, 106
Antimacassar, 33

Baby jacket, 94
Baby shawl, 98
Babywear, 92–99
Bag, 23
Balls, 79, 103, 104
Base chain. See Stitches
Basket, 111
Bathmat, 82
Bathroom, 80–87
Bed linen edgings, 72
Bedspread, 70
Bedroom, 68–79
Bell, 102
Blanket, 38
Blocking and pressing, 15
Bobble, 110, 119
Bonnet, 96
Bookmark, 30
Boot, 104
Braids, 121–2
Butterflies and flowers chart, 90

Cake band, 62
Canopy and ruffle, 90
Cards, 112–15
Celebration, 102–15
Chain. See Stitches
Changing color, 11
Chest cover. See Tabletop
Christmas, ball, 103; bell, 102; ribbon, 102
Christmas decorations. See Decorations
Christmas tree angel, 106
Christmas tree chart, 14
Circles, 10–11, 34
Coffee jar cover, 47
Cord, 15, 121
Corners, 33–36, 121
Curtains, 18, 84
Cushion, 38, 76

Decorations, 102–10
Decreasing, 10, 13. See also Multiples
Diamond patterns, 59–60, 126
Doily, 58
Door curtain, 18
Double chain, 9
Double crochet. See Stitches
Double triple. See Stitches
Dress, baby, 92
Dressing-table set, 73

Edgings (trim), 117–21
Egg cozy, 48
Embroidered gifts, 40, 112, 114
Equipment, 6

Fastening off, 8
Filet crochet, 11–14; bed linen edgings, 72, 73; door curtain, 18; guest towel edging, 83; insertions, 122; jam jar cover, 50; bassinette trim, 90; practice piece for shaping, 13; shelf edging, 50; techniques, 11–13
Flat-fell seam, 108
Floral card, 112
Flowerpot cover, 21
Flowers, 22, 114, 123, 126; in filet, 12, 14, 90
Frame, 35

Galleon chart, 18
Gloves, 26
Granny squares, 33
Guest towel edging, 83
Guitar chart, 14

Half double. See Stitches
Hall, 17–27
Heart, 104
High-wheeler card, 114
Hooks, 6
Hot water bottle cover, 71

Ice cream cone border, 46
Increasing, 10, 13. See also Multiples
Insertions, 122–6

Jam jar cover, 50

Key bookmark, 30
Kitchen, 44–55

Lace doily, 58
Lacet. See Stitches
Lamp shade, 31
Lavender sachets, 86
Leaves, 21, 22, 112, 119
Living room, 28–43

Motifs, bedspread, 70; canopy and ruffle, 90; key bookmark, 30; napkin ring, 67; picot insertions, 126; snow crystal, 105; sofa throw, 33; tablecloth, 60
Multiples, 6

Napkin ring, 67
Needlecase, 40
Notes, 6
Nursery, 89–99

Picot, edgings, 118, 121; motif, 126; needlecase, 40
Picture frame, 35
Pillowcase edging, 73
Pillow, 38
Pineapple design (pitcher cover), 51–4

Pitcher cover, 51
Place mat, 42
Plant hanging, 54, 55
Playing cards envelope, 32
Popcorn motif, 67, 71
Pot holders, 54
Pressing, 15
Purse, 20

Ribbon, 102
Rose chart, 12
Rug, 49

Sewing, 15
Shamrock design, 21
Shaping, 10, 13
Shawls, 23, 98
Sheet edging, 72
Shelf edging, 50
Single crochet, 8
Slipknot, 7
Snow crystal, 105
Snowman, 109
Sofa throw, 33
Spider flower, 58–59, 123
Spirals, 10–11, 55
Stiffening, 109, 111
Stitches, 7–9; chain, 7, 9; double chain, 9; double crochet, 9; half double, 8; lacet, 13, 83; single crochet, 8; slip stitch, 8, 121; triple, 9; triple double, 9

Table center, 42
Tablecloth, 60
Table runner, 19
Tabletop (chest cover), 74
Tassel, 75
Tea cozy, 63
Teapot chart, 14
Tea time, 56–67
Techniques, 6, 7–15
Tension, 6
Tissue box cover, 87
Toilet tissue cover, 82
Towel edging, 83
Tower Bridge chart, 51
Tray cloth, 59
Triangles, 46, 118
Trimmings, 15, 117–26
Turning chains, 6, 9
Twisted cord, 15

Wave pattern, 82
Wheels, 114 122
Windows pillow, 38
Women's gloves, 26
Working in rounds, 10–11

Yarns, 6, 127